BLUE RIBBON LAW

BLUE RIBBON LAW

THE INDISPENSABLE GUIDE FOR HORSE OWNERS, HORSE PROPERTY OWNERS, AND TRAINERS

POLLY HEY, J.D.

FOREWORD BY JOHN FRENCH

Polly Hey, J.D.
Info@blueribbonlaw.com
https://www.blueribbonlaw.com/

Blue Ribbon Law, Polly Hey, J.D. —1st ed. ISBN 978-1-955242-61-5

DEDICATION

To my mother, Nancy, whose resilience as a legally blind horse trainer taught me that vision comes from the heart, not just the eyes. Who turned adversity into mastery, training horses and young equestrians with dreams bigger than the sky. Your unwavering belief in me, your steadfast support from the sidelines, and your wisdom in training me as an equestrian and in life have shaped the person I am today. You are the epitome of courage and my number-one cheerleader in life's grand arena.

To my father, Randy, few people are fortunate enough to start their career working side by side with their father, whose legal work was so highly respected by judges and attorneys alike, and to be treated as an equal partner from day one. You've been my greatest mentor both in law and in life. Your footsteps are the ones I aspire to follow, and your wisdom has shaped not only my legal arguments but also the very core of who I am.

And to my children, Timmy and Ellie— You are the light that illuminates my world, each of you shining in your own unique way. I am immeasurably proud of the wonderful young people you've become—compassionate, intelligent, and resilient. May you always chase your dreams as fiercely as the wind chases the mane of a galloping horse.

CONTENTS

PRAISE FOR "BLUE RIBBON LAW"

A Must-Read For Anyone Involved with Horses
"Blue Ribbon Law" is a must-read for anyone involved with horses. Polly Hey gave me insight and direction as my business was failing. I succumbed to bogus arrangements and dishonesty. Yes, I was seriously taken advantage of, but Polly came on board and literally turned everything around. She helped create sound contracts regarding bills of sale, employment, payroll, and boarding. "Blue Ribbon Law" will provide you with correct information, enabling you to enjoy your horses and feel secure.

Leslie Nelson - Owner, Mirador Equestrian, LLC

Polly Dispels Myths and Delivers Simple Solutions
I have known and had the privilege to work with Polly on several occasions. She shares her wealth of knowledge and does not miss a beat. She clearly lays out the risks and pitfalls and gives the reader the tools to mitigate against such risks. She does an excellent job of dispelling the myths and keeping it simple. As an Equine Insurance specialist, horse owner, and competitor, I will be recommending her book to all my clients who own and work with horses. It's always a pleasure to work with Polly and to find the right solution for fellow horse owners and enthusiasts.

Tom Rattigan - Equine Practice Leader

An Important Book for Horse Professionals of All Calibers
"Blue Ribbon Law" is an important book for young professionals and for well-established professionals as well. It is imperative that we all educate ourselves in the areas expertly outlined in this book. I have over 30 years of experience as a professional, and I'm still learning every day. With the cost of horses, owning horses, and running a horse-related business today, it is our responsibility to our clients and ourselves to be armed with some legal knowledge and to have the wisdom to keep a professional lawyer in our corner to advise and protect us.

Laura Mayfield Gerst - Owner/Trainer, Windy Hill Equestrian, Inc.

Buy Five Copies Right Now

This is absolutely a must-read for every equine lover! As an attorney who grew up with horses, I saw first-hand how many times horse owners and property owners could have avoided problems had they known even just a little bit about the law. Don't just buy 1 copy… BUY 5 and gift them to people you know. Polly Hey does an incredible job of breaking down the law and helping you understand what to look out for and what to do, to do it right the first time.

Kristen David - CEO and Founder, Upleveling Your Business

A Goldmine of Guidance and Advice – A Must-Have Reference

Polly has been instrumental in helping me navigate running a successful equestrian business. I started my journey with Polly over 10 years ago and she is a wealth of knowledge in regards to safeguarding your investment whether it be your equestrian property, business, or just owning a horse. She is a horsewoman herself so she truly understands the ins and outs and can foresee lots of the unexpected pitfalls equestrians don't. This book is a goldmine of all of her wonderful guidance and advice in one place for quick reference or a deep dive before you decide if owning horses or an equestrian business is for you. There are so many unknowns when it comes to the equestrian lifestyle, especially in California, and the internet provides us with so much misinformation every equestrian should have this book in their arsenal of resources. Clear, concise, and readable — an absolute must-have.

Aimee Davis - Owner of Flyin D Livestock, Chino Hills, CA

Got a Horse? Get the Book

"Blue Ribbon Law" is a must-read for everyone involved in Equestrian sports. As a lifelong equestrian, investor, and now facility owner, I found this clear, concise, and beautifully organized book invaluable! I have already identified some areas for improvement in safeguarding myself and my business. As one who has also only narrowly escaped significant loss after a "handshake" deal, I stand wholeheartedly behind Ms. Hey's warnings. Want a horse? Got a horse? Get the book. Get a lawyer and get yourself protected!

Mary Jo Tisor Kaplan - Founder and CEO, Kaplan Consulting, LLC

"Blue Ribbon Law" Culminates Years of Problem Solving

Polly started as a friend and fellow competitor when we were juniors. In my 25 years as a professional in this business, she has been my go-to for all my legal questions, contracts, and consulting. This book is culmination of years of solving all the problems you don't see coming in this business and everything you would like to prevent from happening to you. Whether you are a parent, horse owner, trainer, barn owner, salesman, independent contractor, or any type of horse enthusiast, there is something in here you will benefit from reading. Polly uses real problems that have arisen over her years in business and offers solutions. More importantly, she warns you about the protection you need so you don't get in the same predicament. Most professionals as well as horse owners in general know they want to minimize their risk but they often don't understand the risks nor how to protect themselves from them. This book talks in real terms about real situations and provides clear suggestions on the best plans to prevent as well as remedy them in some cases. "We all believe that the worst won't happen to us until it does" she explains. This book is not only educational for all level of horsemen but helps you prevent the worst-case scenario which unfortunately can happen all too easily in this business.

Hope Hobday Glynn - Horse Trainer, Horse salesman, Clinician

FOREWORD BY JOHN FRENCH

I've known Polly and her family for thirty years, going back to when her mother's training business in the Bay Area was five minutes down the road from my own business, Waldenbrook Farm. Polly's mother, Nancy, specialized in training young children on ponies. She gave them a strong foundation for riding, so if they chose to continue in the sport, they would have the tools they needed to become successful riders.

With this book, Polly is following in her mother's footsteps and giving people in the horse industry the foundation they need to protect themselves, their clients, and their horses.

Polly has been my attorney, and she's helped me more times than I can count. Thanks to Polly's work, I've been protected from and prepared for any situation that could arrive, and I've recommended her to many clients over the years. Yet, there was a time in my career when I didn't understand the importance of having a lawyer in my corner…

The horse industry does business on a handshake too often. This can lead to real problems for everyone involved. You can be an honest person and try to do everything right, but if you have nothing in writing, there's a high risk that something could go wrong.

I have had to learn this the "hard way" several times early in my career. There have been times when I didn't realize I needed legal protections in place until it was too late. If you aren't prepared for these incidents, they can be frustrating to navigate.

I'm a rider—that's what I do best. I'm not a lawyer. I needed someone with legal expertise to look out for me so I could focus on riding and training horses. Since I began working with Polly, I've never had to worry about contracts, insurance, or collecting payments. I know that if anything goes wrong, Polly has prepared my business in the best way possible. Polly has helped many of my clients deal with sales that went bad or horse property issues, and it puts me at ease knowing that my clients have someone to turn to when they encounter challenges.

Whether you own one horse or a large business, you need to be protected. And if you're dealing with horses, your regular attorney just won't do. You need someone who specializes in equine law. If you go to the lawyer down the road who knows the law but doesn't understand the horse industry, you may not be as protected as you think you are.

Embracing the insights from Polly's book and getting legal advice now can serve as insurance for your future financial and reputational well-being. Riding horses can be a dangerous sport. Things happen...But when you've prepared for possible risks alongside a trusted equine lawyer, you can have peace of mind that you won't get any big surprises later on.

If we want to protect ourselves, our clients, and our horses, we need an expert like Polly to teach us the foundation of legal issues that can affect our industry.

HOW TO USE THIS BOOK

This book has been crafted to facilitate quick and straightforward access to crucial information for anyone involved in the equine industry. Whether you're a horse owner, horse property manager, trainer, a family office dealing with horse management and property, or part of a horse association or regulatory body, this book is specifically tailored to cater to your needs.

To best accomplish this, after Chapter 1, the book is divided into the following sections: Horse Owners, Horse Property Owners, Trainers, Family Offices, and Horse Associations and Governing Bodies.

I recommend everyone read the Introduction and Chapter 1, then, jump to the section that is most useful for your current needs. Once you've read the section that applies to you, don't skip the Conclusion. It's filled with extra insights, specialized resources for those navigating the horse industry, and a special gift reserved for you. Keep this book on your bookshelf as a ready reference.

You'll notice that I may repeat information across sections. For example, if you are both a horse owner and a horse property owner, you may find some of the same information stated in both sections. This book is intended to be a reference tool that is easy to open up when you have a question or are facing a challenge. I wanted to make the relevant ideas easily accessible in each chapter so you won't have to search the whole book to find what you need.

★ **Horse Owners read Chapters 2 through 6**

★ **Horse Property Owners read Chapters 7 through 9**

★ **Trainers read Chapter 6 and Chapter 10**

★ **Family Offices: Read the sections for Horse Owners (Chapters 2 through 6), Horse Property Owners (Chapters 7 through 9), then read Chapter 11 on issues specific to Family Offices**

★ **Horse Associations and Governing Bodies read Chapter 12**

In writing this book, my ultimate objective for you centers around three key pillars: **Clarity, Awareness, and Understanding**.

First, I want you to gain **clarity** concerning what could happen and how those risks could impact you, as well as the proactive steps you can take to prevent them.

Second, I want you to cultivate an **awareness** regarding the legal best practices that can serve you so that when an issue does arise, you are more equipped to handle it and are not relying on outdated methods.

Third, I want you to **understand** the frequent pitfalls you may run into so that you can ask good questions to your legal counsel and make informed decisions as you proceed.

This book uses a combination of fictionalized scenarios and real case law to illustrate concepts, but all of these stories reflect common situations our office has faced over the years. Though some situations have been fictionalized to maintain confidentiality, remember that every story is based on real events; any of these situations could happen to you.

INTRODUCTION

If you have opened this book, either you're a horse enthusiast or someone close to you shares this passion. Raised in a family deeply ingrained in the horse industry, I know firsthand the joy and richness that equestrian life can bring. My mother, a seasoned horse trainer, introduced me to riding when I was barely six months old, letting me share the saddle with her. By the tender age of three, I was already riding solo.

Throughout my youth, I had the privilege of competing at Hunter/Jumper shows, winning multiple championships, including the NorCal Senior Medal Finals. Although I've stepped back from the competitive scene to support my twins in their own riding endeavors, I continue to ride our three horses. Equestrian law is more than just my career... I have a deep, lifelong love of horses.

As rewarding as it is, the equestrian industry holds many hidden dangers that you may not become aware of until it's too late. As the daughter of a trainer, I witnessed so many unfortunate incidents that could have been prevented with the right protections in place. I decided to practice equine law to help the equestrian community understand and avoid risk, prevent misfortune, and navigate the legal complexities of the industry so we can focus on the joy of riding horses.

The traditions of the equestrian industry often encourage people to operate on trust and do business "on a handshake." That mindset sounds friendly and idealistic, but it often leaves you unprotected. Even if business is done with more than a "handshake," many are misinformed about the proper contracts and insurance necessary to avoid serious legal and financial consequences.

Without the right protections in place before a dispute arises, not only can you be impacted by liability and the potential financial loss it can bring, but you may also find yourself with big legal bills and, in some instances, could even face criminal charges. The fear and stress that I have seen put upon someone because of a horse-related dispute or accident is enormous.

In most cases, legal disputes do not have to end in disaster for either party. There are actions people can take to protect themselves from liability, but too few people are informed about the common risks and their preventive measures.

After over two decades of practicing law and witnessing firsthand the impact of being unprepared for disputes or accidents, I decided to take action and educate people about the risks they face and what they can do to mitigate the risks. This book is a byproduct of that mission. By the time you're done reading, you can expect to have a better understanding of the potential liabilities you face and what you can do to protect yourself.

When you're aware of the common legal risks in the equestrian industry and their solutions, you can avoid misunderstandings and reduce or eliminate the risk of a lawsuit. When you're protected, you can live with confidence and freedom from worry, knowing that even if something goes wrong, you, your business, and your family will weather the storm. You can turn your focus back to what you care about—horses.

If you're in the industry long enough, sooner or later, you're likely to face a problem. Maybe a horse transaction will go awry, and you'll realize your faulty contract leaves you with no options for recourse. Maybe an accident on your property will lead to a lawsuit you never saw coming. If you're a trainer, maybe a dispute with a training client will wreak havoc on the business you've worked for years to build. In any of these situations, having simple protections in place can help you avoid disaster. Over the years, I've watched many people in the industry express regret after they discover they could have taken action to prevent a legal dispute. None of these people are to blame for not taking preventative action—no one had informed them of the risks, so they had no idea that they were exposed to liability until an incident occurred. It's my hope to change that.

My wish for you the reader of this book is that:

- You'll gain clarity about the risks you face and the steps you can take now to protect yourself.
- You'll build an awareness of legal best practices so that if you do face a problem, you'll know how to seek proper legal guidance instead of doing things "the way they've always been done."
- You'll understand common pitfalls so you can ask good questions of your attorney and make informed choices as you move forward.

In the following pages, you'll read about the key information anyone involved in the industry should know about common legal risks and how they can be mitigated. With this information at your disposal, you'll be able to safeguard against liability, live free from fear, and enjoy a rewarding life in the equestrian community.

CHAPTER ONE

The Risks You Don't Know You Face

The Horse Owner

Lisa and John pick up their ten-year-old daughter, Jessica, from a birthday party at a local stable. On the drive home, they hear endless, enthusiastic chatter from the backseat as Jessica goes on and on about her pony ride.

Over the next few weeks, all she wants to talk about is horses. She makes up names for hypothetical ponies she wants her parents to buy, she plays "horse jumping" in the backyard, and she asks the pressing question, "Can I start riding lessons?" Lisa and John are nervous–they don't know anything about the equestrian world, they wonder if it's dangerous for children to ride, and they give themselves headaches Googling the cost of entering the sport. But Lisa and John don't want to disappoint their daughter, and they don't want to ignore her newfound interest.

Lisa gets in touch with a local stable and signs Jessica up for lessons. A few years pass, and what seemed at first like a child's whim has turned into a dedication to the sport. Jessica's trainer tells her parents that if she wants to advance to the next level and compete, the family will have to lease or buy a horse.

Lisa and John are excited to take this next step and help their daughter succeed, but they feel a bit overwhelmed. This isn't a hobby like any other hobby... They're not just buying their daughter soccer cleats or ballet shoes. They're buying a living, breathing animal. How will they protect this huge investment?

The Trainer

Robert grew up in the equestrian world, and the sport is his lifeblood. He became a trainer so he could spend every day around the animals he loves. Now, he has a thriving training business. To Robert, there's no greater joy than spending a day at the stables riding, helping a new rider make a breakthrough, or overcoming challenges at a competition.

But what Robert doesn't know is that he has a huge liability risk...

When he began his career as a trainer, he modeled his practices and processes after the people who mentored and trained him. But these people were just following in the footsteps of their mentors... And those mentors were just following in the footsteps of their predecessors... The result is that many trainers do things the way that everyone has done them for 100 years. The equestrian industry is steeped in tradition. Sometimes, this can be one of the beautiful things about it, but when it comes to business practices, trainers may not realize that the way they operate is behind the times. Doing things "the way they've always been done" could leave trainers open to serious liabilities, cost them a significant amount of money, or cost them their livelihood.

It's only natural that Robert wouldn't realize this. He's a trainer. His unique gift is training horses, not running a business. He spends more time thinking about the horses he's training than the contracts he's dealing with. That's perfectly normal... Horses are what he's passionate about, and he's skilled at working with them. But if he doesn't learn the basics about the legal risks that trainers face, one incident could threaten the business he loves and worked so hard to build.

The Horse Property Owner

Most horse property owners start their journeys as horse owners. After years of boarding his daughter's horses at training facilities, John thinks, "Wait a minute. It would be much more cost-effective to keep the horses on our property than to board them." John envisions an idyllic life living on a large, pastoral property with a stable, and he gets his wife, Lisa, on board with the idea. They even hatch a plan to form a passive income stream by letting other riders board horses on their property. The family finds a beautiful property with the house of their dreams... But if they jump into this venture without considering the liabilities of owning a horse property and how to protect against them, they could be setting themselves up for financial disaster.

The Family Office

Rachel runs a successful family office and manages wealth for several high-net-worth families. But when her client, the Johnson family, acquires horses and wants to house them in a stable on their multimillion-dollar property, Rachel realizes she might be heading into unfamiliar territory. Horses are living assets, and they're unlike any other asset Rachel has managed before. Rachel has never been involved in the equestrian world and isn't sure what owning horses entails. "But I've bought and sold companies before," she thinks, "How complicated could a horse be?"

The answer is that a horse is a far, far more complicated asset than it seems. When Rachel has acquired any other asset, she's turned to experts to guide her decisions. Why should a horse be any different? If Rachel wants to manage and protect her client's assets in the best way possible, it's in her best interest to understand the risks of horse ownership so she can serve the family successfully. She should also be familiar with the best practices to follow when the family is buying, selling, or leasing their horses.

Preventing Disaster

The vast majority of people become involved in the industry because they, or someone they love, love horses. The industry can be a wonderful community that brings joy to your life... But sometimes, your love of horses can blind you to reality. Your passion and excitement can lead you to make decisions that are not in your economic best interest.

I'm going to guide you through some of the pitfalls you'll face if you have a long enough career in this industry–and I'm going to show you how a little preparation and forethought can save you from easily preventable disasters.

The "Handshake" Problem

The horse industry is centuries old. For most of that long history, deals were made on a handshake…

Today, many people *still* make deals on a handshake—and this causes many of the problems in the industry.

Whether it's a sale, a lease, a boarding agreement, a training agreement, an agreement between a trainer and their employee, an agreement between a horse property owner and an employee, or an agreement between a horse property owner and a trainer, making these types of agreements on nothing more than a handshake can lead to serious trouble.

A large portion of the horse industry refuses to use the same sound business practices that are used in any other industry. Would a businessperson make a multimillion-dollar deal on a handshake? Would a doctor refuse to comply with state regulation codes? These reckless practices would be considered ludicrous in any other industry. Yet so many in the horse industry don't think through the liability issues they face by not complying with normal business practices.

Handshake deals used to work. In the era when horses were a widespread mode of transportation, owning a horse was very common and cost less. If something went wrong with the deal, there was less risk because there was less money at stake. Horses were historically used for transportation and labor, but now, they're used for sport and pleasure. This has dramatically increased their value.

Now, horses can sell for tens of thousands of dollars…hundreds of thousands of dollars…even several million dollars.

A horse is now the equivalent of an elite professional athlete. It may receive expensive treatments such as magnetic blankets or vibrating floors, similar to the way Olympic athletes receive care.

And a horse is a unique asset because it's a live animal. It's different from owning other expensive assets like a car or a house. There are many more variables at play that could put you at risk.

If you buy a Ferrari believing it's in mint condition, but you drive it a few times and realize you were sold a Ferrari with a bad tire, you can get the tire fixed. Horses don't work that way…

If your horse has an injury or another health condition the seller didn't disclose, there's no quick fix like replacing a tire. You may not be able to use the horse for the activities that you bought it for, and if you don't have a well-drafted contract, you may not be able to get your money back.

Without a contract, nothing is in writing, so if you're sold something that doesn't live up to what you were promised, you have no proof that that is the case. You made a deal on a handshake, and now you have to live with the consequences…

Many horse owners unknowingly bet $50,000, $100,000, even $1,000,000 on a handshake.

Most people would agree that it's a bad decision to bet a million dollars on a handshake, but that's essentially what many horse owners unknowingly do. These horse owners don't even realize that they're being reckless or foolish—handshake deals are so ingrained into the horse industry that they don't even question what they're doing.

In our industry, the connections run deep, and it's not uncommon to hear someone say, "Why would I need a contract? I've known this person's family for years. I trust them. They stand behind what they do. What if I suggest a contract and they think I'm implying that I don't trust them?" or "Will I make my trainer upset if I suggest I want an attorney to draft the contract? Will it cause tension in our relationship?"

These owners don't realize that *both parties* are at significant risk when a deal is made on a handshake. Even if both parties have the best intentions, we're dealing with live animals, and the unexpected can happen. If you trust and/or have a personal relationship with the other party, that's all the more reason to avoid a handshake deal and seek out a contract that will protect both sides.

The handshake has evolved...

California Business and Professions Code § 19525 requires a written contract for the sale of a horse. Many people now realize that they need some level of a written agreement, but many of these agreements are no better than a handshake. The "modern handshake" is a contract that isn't properly prepared.

Many people attempt to draft contracts themselves. But what happens if you have a "DIY" contract and something goes wrong? DIY contracts often have so many ambiguities that you would likely need to go to court to resolve them or just take a loss and walk away.

When people create DIY contracts, they usually leave out important details because they don't know what to consider. For example, when drafting a co-ownership agreement, a DIY-er may not consider questions such as: Who decides what classes the horse competes in? If it's a 50/50 co-ownership and the contract doesn't specify this, a disagreement between the co-owners could end up in court.

It's very common for those in the horse industry to use form contracts that can be found online or to copy and paste from a contract that someone they know used previously.

The problem with doing this is that attorneys draft a contract based on the best interests of a specific client. If this contract then gets passed around to others to be modified or reused, these people may be signing something that doesn't represent their best interests because it was drafted for someone else's unique situation.

For example, a contract you get from a friend may have been originally drafted for someone in Texas, but you're trying to use it in California. The law varies from state to state and county to county. If you use a contract that was not written for the laws specific to where you live, you could be at risk.

And if each new user of the contract makes small modifications to fit their needs, it's like playing "telephone" with the contract. You end up with a "Frankenstein contract" that's been modified so many times that it no longer makes sense. Is this the type of contract you want standing between you and a million-dollar lawsuit? A contract prepared without an attorney is as good as a handshake...

Ignorance is Bliss

Bad contracts may make you sleep easier at night ("I signed a contract, what could go wrong?"), but many don't discover that the contract they think protects them is full of holes until the worst happens.

Often, you're not aware of the risk you're in until it's too late.

Most people in the horse industry know there is some risk, but they may not fully grasp how significant that risk could be. They often have "it can't happen to me" syndrome. We all believe that the worst won't happen to us—until it does.

We all believe that the worst won't happen to us—until it does.

Many horse owners or trainers believe that because they haven't had a problem in the past there won't ever be a problem. They say, "But I've used this contract 5 times before; what could possibly go wrong?" It only takes one problem to become very costly...

If you're a first-time horse buyer, the risk is magnified because you don't know what you don't know. Without experience in the industry, it's hard to fully grasp what the risks are and that can cost first-time owners thousands of dollars and years in court.

For example, someone new to the industry may not realize that if they are leasing a horse and it gets hurt, they may not be able to return it unless their contract provides for a return or replacement in case of injury.

Sellers need legal protection, too. Some people erroneously believe, "I'm the seller. I don't need a contract. What could go wrong on my end?" What happens if your contract doesn't have an as-is clause and the buyer later discovers a health problem with the horse that you didn't know about? You could be liable for a large sum when you could have been easily protected by a thorough contract.

Even sophisticated people can lose big time...

Jess Jackson, a billionaire entrepreneur who founded the Kendall-Jackson Winery, was a successful trial attorney and owned racehorses. When Jackson was buying horses, the California law in effect at that time required a written bill of sale but was limited in scope and the amount of damages that could be recovered. His agents were making every transaction on a handshake...and Jackson was defrauded out of millions of dollars. Because of this, Jackson lobbied for laws that required a written bill of sale and other legal protections, including disclosure of dual agency, treble damages, and expansion of the law to

> apply to all horse transactions, not just racehorses.
> I was fortunate to be a part of the effort to get this
> legislation passed.
>
> If it can happen to a savvy billionaire entrepreneur, it
> can happen to you...

As in all situations in life, you can navigate problems better if you're informed. Participating in the horse industry can bring great joy to your life, but I've also seen people experience stress, tragedy, and financial ruin because they didn't inform themselves of the possible risks.

The good news is that there are actionable steps you can take to avoid risk so you can let go of worry and enjoy your life in the horse industry—but before you take these steps, you need to become aware of what you're missing.

In the following chapters, I'm going to show each horse industry demographic the most pressing risks they're likely to face and how you can take action to prevent risk.

Though most of these stories are amalgamations of common situations I've seen people face throughout my career, the important thing to remember is that none of these stories had to have a terrible ending. Disaster usually could have been avoided if someone had put the right protections in place. Life is unpredictable, but if you take preventative measures against risk, you can avoid or diminish the effect of a worst-case scenario.

CHAPTER 2

Horse Owners - Overcoming Challenges with Horse Transactions

When you buy anything, you may face the age-old sales problem...

Your purchase doesn't live up to your expectations.

This can happen with anything you buy, from a new shirt to a car to a house. Buyer's remorse intensifies the more money you spend...

Swallowing a Six-Figure Loss

A client in Southern California wanted to buy a high-level jumper. She found a horse from Europe on the internet that she liked. The seller sent her videos, she had the horse vetted, and then she bought the horse for six figures. But when the horse arrived, it couldn't do what it had done in the videos. The client felt strongly that the horse in the video, the horse she thought she was buying, had been substituted for a similar-looking horse. She believed she bought one horse, but she got another... And this horse lacked some of the abilities of the horse she wanted. Because she had already gone through with the deal, her only remedy would be to hire a European lawyer and attempt to get her money refunded. After realizing how difficult this process would be, she decided to accept her six-figure loss.

When you're buying a horse, the chances of not having your expectations met are higher because a horse is a living animal. A seller may know the horse's previous behavior and health, but these factors could change unexpectedly. Whether you're a buyer or a seller, the unpredictable nature of dealing with a live animal can have enormous financial consequences and requires legal protection…especially if you're new to the industry, have never bought a horse before, and are unsure what to expect.

This is exactly the position Lisa and John are in when they begin looking to buy a horse for their daughter, Jessica. Their only point of exposure to the industry so far is through their daughter's riding lessons, but they don't know much about horses. During the buying process, there are many details that an experienced equestrian might catch that Lisa and John are likely to miss because they're new to the industry.

For example, an experienced equestrian would know that a horse may be great in one training program or environment but not in another. Yet, this thought may never occur to Lisa and John. If they buy a horse that has a successful record, they may be disappointed to find that it doesn't have the same success when moved to their trainer's program. Also, since they're buying a horse for a young rider, the horse's performance may differ when Jessica rides it and when an older rider with decades of experience rides it. Sometimes, even moving a horse from one climate to another can affect its performance. If Lisa and John don't consider this before a purchase, they may be disappointed when the horse doesn't live up to their expectations.

On top of their inexperience, Lisa and John are in another vulnerable position–they're buying a horse for their daughter. When people buy horses for their children, the emotional stakes of wanting to make their child happy can cloud their rational thinking and lead to poor decisions. If the horse doesn't live up to their child's expectations, it can be devastating. John and Lisa would do anything to make Jessica happy, and they wanted to buy her a horse to give her an amazing experience and help her advance to the next stage of the sport she loves. Their fear of disappointing her makes it difficult for Lisa and John to make clear judgments throughout the process of purchasing a horse.

After looking at several horses, John and Lisa find a horse that Jessica adores. It meets all of the specifications they were looking for, and it has a promising record. They decide to tell the seller that they're interested and will go home to think it over for a few days before finalizing the purchase. But when they tell the seller they're interested, the seller says, "If you go home and think it over, the horse won't be here when you get back. I have five interested parties coming to see the horse later this afternoon, and I can't hold the horse for you. If you want this horse, you need to make a decision now."

"I guess horse sales move fast," John says to Lisa. The couple would never make a decision this quickly if they were purchasing a car or house, but because they've never bought a horse before, they assume that this is just the pace of the industry.

John and Lisa don't want to lose this seemingly perfect horse, and Jessica has already become attached to it, so despite their hesitations, they purchase the horse.

In the horse industry, it's common for transactions to be high-pressure and fast-paced. Buyers are often told, as John and Lisa were, that they need to make a decision because there are other interested parties waiting to swoop in and buy the horse if they go home to think it over. You may only get the opportunity to ride the horse once or twice before you're expected to decide if you want to buy it or not. You're told you need to sign the contract today or you'll lose the horse, leaving you no time to get a vet check or verify records. You're putting a lot of trust into the seller, and it can feel overwhelming.

Sometimes, there are other interested parties ready to make the transaction quickly, but often, this is a false pressure applied as a tactic to close a deal. When you're looking to buy a horse, you need to be prepared to walk away if the seller tries to pressure you.

It may not feel like it, but there's always another horse. Yes, you may lose the opportunity to own this horse, but it's better to seek out another horse than to purchase a horse under pressure and later find out you didn't have all the facts. You may even find a better horse by turning down a horse from a seller who tries to rush you.

In my experience, buyers don't learn to walk away until they've been burned once or twice and have lost a lot of money. Do yourself a favor, skip the pain of learning from a bad experience, and walk away from any horse sale that doesn't allow you time to follow the proper procedures.

Buying a Horse for a Child

I understand why many buyers fall prey to false sales pressure. Buying a horse can be a highly emotional process, especially if the horse is for your child. It can be hard to say "no" and disappoint your child if they fall in love with a particular horse.

But you have to remember how high the stakes are when you're purchasing a horse. If your child is going to ride the horse, you need to get as much information as possible to ensure that this horse will be safe to ride.

Children aren't great at critical thinking. Your ten-year-old daughter might get excited about a horse, but she isn't able to think about veterinary records, contracts, and potential lawsuits.

It may be difficult in the moment to break your child's heart and walk away from a horse they've fallen in love with, but remember that you're ultimately looking out for your child's safety when you take the time to collect more information about a horse.

Key Considerations for a Sales Contract

California Business and Professions Code Section §19525 states that any sale, purchase, or transfer of an equine must be accompanied by a written bill of sale that sets forth the purchase price and is signed by both the purchaser and the seller or their duly authorized agents.

There are some key elements that need to be in the sales agreement to benefit both the buyer and the seller.

1. **Parties involved in the sale**
   Your contract must include the individuals or entities involved in the transaction, typically the buyer and the seller. The agreement should clearly state their full names and contact information.

2. **Specific Identification of Horse**
   Your contract should include a thorough description of the horse, including microchip number, age, height, and color. It may seem obvious, but ideally, the horse should be specifically identified with a microchip. I have seen multiple instances where a horse arrived, and the buyer discovered it had been substituted for a different horse. If the identification is included in the contract, the buyer can prove that this was the case.

3. **Purchase Price**
   A contract needs a clear specification of the purchase price. When will it be paid? Will it be paid in installments? If the horse will be paid for in installments, you'll need to register

with the UCC so if the buyer goes bankrupt you can have priority in bankruptcy court.

4. **Pre-Purchase Veterinary Exam Language**
   If the buyer had a pre-purchase veterinary exam done, the contract should include a statement that the horse has had a pre-purchase exam done and that the buyer was satisfied with the exam. If a buyer returns two weeks later, claiming the horse is lame, the seller can refute it by proving that the buyer was satisfied with the pre-purchase veterinary exam.

   It is critical that the pre-purchase exam be completed by an independent veterinarian who does not work for the seller and who has not treated the horse previously.

5. **As-Is Language**
   As-Is language states that the seller is selling the horse as it is on the day of the transaction. If the horse develops an unforeseen health problem a week after the sale, the seller won't be liable because they sold the horse as it was on the day of the sale.

6. **Commissions**
   Will any commissions be paid? Is anyone acting as a dual agent? To comply with California law (Business and Professions Code §19525), you need to include this information in a contract. As an attorney, I have represented trainers who have not disclosed commissions, and in the resulting litigation, we were in a weak negotiating position simply because my client hadn't complied with the law, despite it being common knowledge what the commission amounted to—it was just not explicitly stated in the contract.

Some other states have similar laws, so if you are outside of California, I encourage you to check your state statutes before entering into a contract.

7. **Representations and Warranties**
   The seller often provides assurances about the horse's health and condition. These may include claims about the horse's health, training level, temperament, and potential defects or issues. These representations and warranties can play a critical role if disputes arise later, and to be enforceable, they must be included in the Sales Contract.

8. **Title**
   The seller warrants that they own the horse and are the sole owner. This is crucial because there is no title registry for the ownership of a horse—ownership is only determined by the documents you have. If there's an ownership dispute and a title is missing from your contract, you'll have a difficult time proving that you own the horse. There have been cases where a horse was co-owned, and one party sold it without consulting the other. This complicated matters for the new buyer when the other owner came back into the picture, claiming to still be a legal owner of the horse.

9. **Resolving Disputes**
   If there is a dispute between buyer and seller, how will you solve it? Will you go through the court system? The court process can be lengthy, expensive, and public. I recommend that most buyers and sellers include an alternative dispute resolution provision so they can resolve disputes confidentially, and more quickly than through the court. Mediation often gives the parties an opportunity to settle

the case at a fraction of the cost of litigation. Almost every contract I write includes mediation because it's the most painless and cost-effective way to resolve disputes.

10. Risk of Loss Before Delivery

The agreement should stipulate who bears the risk of any harm or loss that might occur to the horse before the buyer takes possession. Typically, the risk remains with the seller until the horse is delivered to the buyer.

11. Date of Delivery

This is the agreed-upon date when the horse will be handed over to the buyer. This can include details about the location and method of delivery.

12. Trial Period

The chances that you will get a trial period are low, but it's usually worth asking. If you do get a trial period, it's one of the trickiest clauses to have in a contract. If something goes wrong in a trial period, who bears responsibility for it? There are dangers in the trial period for both the buyer and the seller. What happens if the horse acts up and injures the potential buyer? What happens if the horse gets injured? Trial periods can be challenging to negotiate because the risk is so high—if something happens to the horse, it can be ambiguous who bears the responsibility for the horse. A well-drafted contract should clarify which party is responsible for incidents that may occur.

Buyer's Checklist

Below, we've compiled a buyer's checklist to be utilized when considering the purchase of a horse. While this list is far from comprehensive, and additional items may need to be incorporated, it addresses some of the top issues we have encountered when clients have a sales agreement dispute. For a downloadable version of this checklist and others, be sure to scan the QR code at the end of the book.

☑ Did the buyer ride the horse in person, or was the buyer only provided with videos?

☑ Did the buyer have an independent vet do a pre-purchase veterinary exam? (An independent vet does not work for the seller and has not seen the horse before)

☑ Did the buyer ask for and receive the horse's previous veterinary records?

☑ Did the buyer look at the horse's show record and verify what the seller stated regarding the horse's success? Did the buyer check for any gaps in the show record? (Gaps could indicate a potential problem.)

☑ Did the buyer ensure the seller warranted a clear title to the horse?

☑ Did the buyer use a well-drafted sales contract?

A Vet Check Cautionary Tale

Amy contacted her daughter's trainer, who was also a local horse broker, to help her find a horse suitable for her daughter, Sophie. The trainer used her network of personal and professional contacts and located a horse that was a 14-year-old warmblood gelding. Sophie and the trainer watched the horse perform at a horse show. At the horse show, Sophie was allowed to try the horse. The trial went well, and the parties agreed that the next step would be a pre-purchase examination by a vet to determine the horse's health and its ability to perform for its intended use.

Amy hired a vet that was part of a big vet clinic. This vet had presented herself to Amy and Sophie as an equine lameness specialist, a statement that was even included in her biography on the vet's website. The vet went about conducting the pre-purchase exam. She did a physical exam as well as radiographs. Amy was present for part of the pre-purchase exam. Throughout the exam, the vet was making complimentary remarks about the horse, including his past performance and medical history, all of which indicated he would be able to perform well for Sophie.

During the pre-purchase exam, Amy asked about doing a drug test, and the vet advised against it, saying it wasn't worth it because if illegal drugs had been administered, it likely wouldn't show up anyways. The horse had some special shoes called "onion shoes," which are a thicker shoe that has a bar across the middle. In general, vets take shoes off a horse when performing X-rays. This vet decided not to take off the shoes for the radiographs, explaining that it was not necessary to get a proper image.

Following the end of the pre-purchase exam, the vet orally communicated her findings to Amy. She said the horse had never been lame before, the horse had some arthritis symptoms that were typical for a horse of that age and not a cause for concern, the radiographs were normal and would show nothing that would cause concern, the horse was well suited for intended use, and the horse's medical history was free from prior issues. Amy didn't have any veterinary training or knowledge, so she relied on the vet's statements.

After the vet discussed the exam with Amy, the vet completed a written pre-purchase form with different information than what was communicated orally to Amy. The written form said the horse was not receiving any drugs. It also said that the horse had been lame before as a result of a right leg strain. A few years before, the horse had had injections in its hocks, stifles, and coffin joints. There was a section on the form that described the horse's physical appearance, and it described that the horse had a low heel in the left forelimb. It noted that there was a superficial injury to the right leg. There was a section that asked if all of these issues were within normal limits, and the vet had written yes, except for that on one of the legs, the horse had a splint, but no other observations or concerns were noted. In the section on this form that talked about the physical exam, it said that the horse was graded a 1 out of 5 for lameness in both of its hind legs. There was no lameness noted in the left front leg or any of the other legs.

At the end, it said the horse was a healthy horse suitable for the 2 foot 6 hunters, was balanced well, and wouldn't make any changes to the front feet. The form did say the horse would need to get its stifles joints injected (and hock joints as needed). This form that the vet filled out was not given to Amy until well after the exam was completed and after the purchase was completed.

Within weeks of the purchase, the horse started to show signs of lameness in its front leg, and at that point, Amy contacted the vet who had originally seen the horse, before the pre-purchase exam. She found out that this vet had treated the horse a few months before her purchase. That vet said that the horse had been lame 3 out of 5 and that the lameness had worsened. That vet also said that when she had removed the shoe from the left front leg, it was very obvious how malformed that foot was.

By this point, Amy had been able to receive the radiographs that she had purchased that the other vet had done during the pre-purchase exam. She had this vet review them, and the vet said that there were multiple problems on the vet records and that she would never recommend buying a horse with radiograph results such as that of this horse. They continued to try to treat the horse, they did an MRI on the horse, and the horse had major issues. None of these issues were ever disclosed by the seller or even noted by the vet who did that pre-purchase when she spoke with Amy.

Amy got a third opinion, and it was determined that the horse was so lame that it needed to be put down. The third opinion vet said that there was no way that these injuries were new and the horse had likely been lame for quite some time. That vet also recommended that Amy should go back and look at the show records to see if there was a period of time that was greater than a few weeks that the horse was not shown. When they did that, they found that the horse had not been shown for eight weeks or longer 14 times over a period of 7 years. One period spanned 55 weeks...

But Amy had already purchased the horse for her daughter, and because she had approved the vet check, she was facing an uphill battle at the possibility of getting her money back, even though the horse was so lame it needed to be put down.

If you're buying a horse, it's crucial that the vet check be conducted by your independent vet—someone you know and trust.

A Caution About Buying a Horse From Europe

Many people now buy horses internationally through the Internet, especially from European sellers. Horses from Europe can be cheaper because there's more land and it's usually cheaper to raise horses there than in the United States.

But if you do this, you may be buying a horse without ever seeing it. When the horse arrives, it may have a vet problem or behavior issues—in some cases, you're given a completely different horse (I've seen it happen...). What do you do? Because you've purchased internationally, you may not have many options.

It's best to prevent this issue by traveling to see the horse if possible. If this isn't possible, send someone you trust to see the horse. If you can't get anyone to see the horse in person, you have no business buying a horse internationally. There's a high risk that something could go wrong, and there aren't many options for recourse if it does.

There are consumer protections in Europe that allow you to return a horse, but it's a long and complicated process. It's not like returning something to Amazon... we're talking about shipping a live animal back overseas. It's expensive and logistically difficult to do. In addition, you would need to get an attorney in Europe. Many people, upon realizing how much of a hassle the return process is, decide it's easier to keep the faulty horse and accept the loss of money.

Another factor that buyers don't consider is that vet records may be in another language. When you send the vet record to your vet at home and they arrive in French or Dutch, what will you do? These are highly technical, complicated documents, and even if you're able to get a translator, they may make a mistake that prevents you from understanding the horse's true condition.

Horse Leases

Horse Leases are common in the horse industry and can offer a family a way to dip their toes in horse ownership without the expensive initial investment. But there are numerous potential problems that could arise with a lease that even many experienced horse professionals don't think about.

Our office has handled multiple cases in which expensive show horses were injured during a lease. If the lease agreement doesn't specify how each party should handle this situation and who bears responsibility, this situation can quickly turn into a complicated dispute...

When lease agreements are borrowed from one person to the next, and people cobble together their own DIY lease agreement, I often see terms being misused because the drafter does not understand the meaning of those terms. One example where this frequently occurs is with the terms lessor and lessee. The lessor is the owner of the horse, and the lessee is the person leasing the horse. This type of mistake can make a lease agreement ambiguous at best, or it can cause significant legal problems.

Mark leased a show horse for his daughter, Lucy. They started with a three-week trial period to determine if the horse was suitable and sound. Then, they had a pre-purchase vet exam done. After the exam was satisfactory, Mark agreed to pay $150,000 for a one-year lease. $100,000 was to be paid at the time they took possession of the horse, and $50,000 was to be paid six months later. The horse showed successfully for the first 3 months of the lease. But after that point, the horse started refusing jumps. The vets did an MRI of the horse, and it turned out the horse had a fracture of its front ankle. The horse underwent surgery and began recovering. At that point, Mark returned the horse to the owners and did not pay the second lease installment. A long lawsuit ensued... Mark believed that the horse's lameness was a preexisting condition and felt he should not have to pay the $50,000. The owner of the horse believed that the horse became injured during the lease and that Mark should pay the $50,000.

The story above is not unusual. Lease disputes are one of the most prevalent types of litigation disputes we see in our office. Had these two parties had a well-drafted contract that stated the remedies if the horse became injured or whether the horse could be returned, they could have avoided a lawsuit.

Key Considerations for Leases

1. **What happens if the horse is injured?**
    If you're the lessee, are you liable if the horse gets injured during the lease? If you're the lessor, do you want the right to have an injured horse returned to you so you can control how its rehab is done?

2. **Can you return the horse early?**
    If the horse is not working out, can you return the horse early and possibly lose your lease fee but no longer pay monthly bills? Is the lessee exempt from the remaining payments if the horse is returned early?

3. **Do you, as the lessee, have the option to buy the horse? What are the terms?**
    If you have the option to buy the horse at the end of the lease term, does the lease fee go toward the purchase price?

4. **Do you have to stay in training with a particular trainer during the lease?**
    An owner may choose to let you lease their horse because they trust the trainer you currently work with. If you decide to switch trainers during the lease, the owner may not be happy, so it's best to clarify these expectations in the contract.

5. **Are there limitations on training and showing to avoid overworking the horse?**
    How often can you show the horse? What classes can you show it in? How high can it jump?

6. **How much is the lease fee?**

   A typical lease fee is 1/3 of the purchase price of the horse per year. For example, a one-year lease of a $100,000 horse would cost about $33,000.

7. **If the lease fee is paid over time, what are the terms and remedies if the lessee doesn't pay a second or third installment?**

   If you are the lessor, you want to spell out the remedies for non-payment in the lease. If you don't include them, you will likely have to take the lessee to court to get the horse back, which is costly and time-consuming.

8. **Does the lease include alternative dispute resolution language or some way to resolve disputes outside of a courtroom?**

   If you can't resolve an issue, are you headed to court or mediation? Does the dispute resolution language protect your privacy, or will any dispute be public record? If you don't include alternative dispute resolution language, your only option is to go to court. If the case goes to court, it all becomes public record.

Show Records

Before purchasing or leasing a horse, it's in your best interest to obtain the horse's show records. A seller may tell you that the horse has won certain awards, but you always want to verify this information. Even if the seller is technically telling the truth, there may be details you'd want to know about.

For example, a buyer was told that a horse ranked highly in a prestigious competition...but it was during the year when the COVID-19 pandemic caused fewer people to compete and lowered the standards of the competition. If the buyer hadn't discovered this detail, they may have been disappointed by the horse's true abilities.

If a horse has a large gap in its show records, it can be a red flag. This could mean the horse was injured during that period of time. This may not dissuade you from buying the horse, but if the seller hasn't disclosed the injury yet, you'll need to get more information about it.

Show records help you see if what you think you're buying is what you're really buying. Look for anomalies, ask questions, and consider your options.

CHAPTER 3

Horse Owners - Avoiding Buyer's Remorse

What happens when the horse you bought isn't the horse you expected? What if the horse is lame or has a health issue you didn't know about? What if the horse behaves in a way you didn't expect based on how it was sold to you?

A Simple, Yet Costly Mistake

Melissa grew up riding, and now that she is settled with a job, she is excited to get back into the sport. She started looking for a horse to buy and even tried a few but hadn't found the "one" until she found Cinnamon online. She reached out to Sally, the seller, who seemed so nice. Sally told Melissa all about Cinnamon and convinced her that Cinnamon was the perfect match she had been seeking. Cinnamon was in Melissa's price range with a purchase price of $12,000. The problem was that Cinnamon was located across the country in Maine, and Melissa lived in California. Sally said not to worry, as she could send Melissa many videos of Cinnamon in different situations and environments. After watching the videos, Melissa proceeded with a pre-purchase veterinary exam, even though she had not seen Cinnamon in person. Sally suggested Melissa use her veterinarian since her veterinarian knew Cinnamon, and Melissa agreed. Cinnamon arrived, and after riding her twice, Melissa discovered that she had spinal issues that made her unrideable. These spinal issues also caused behavioral problems, making riding Cinnamon unsafe. Melissa wanted to return the horse, but unfortunately, nothing could be done because a veterinarian check had been performed, and Melissa had approved the veterinary check in the contract.

Melissa made several mistakes in this transaction. First, she bought a horse off of a video and trusted the seller. Second, she used Sally's veterinarian instead of finding an independent veterinarian. People often mistakenly think that it's best to use the seller's veterinarian because the seller's veterinarian knows the horse well. The seller's veterinarian has a financial stake in maintaining a good relationship with the seller, which encourages future collaborations. This isn't to imply that the seller's veterinarian intentionally conceals the truth, but it can cause a potential conflict of interest that, at the time, seems innocent but may have drastic consequences later.

In this case, Melissa had requested to see Cinnamon's past vet records, and on the day of the pre-purchase exam, the veterinarian's office sent over the records, which included the pre-purchase exam from two years before, when Sally purchased Cinnamon. Unfortunately, Melissa took a quick glance and saw a clean bill of health (from two years prior, not realizing the date) and moved forward with the purchase of Cinnamon that same day. She was so excited to have finally found the "one" that she didn't want to delay. When the current pre-purchase exam report came in a few days later, after the contract had been signed and the spinal issues were discovered, Melissa realized what had happened.

If she had worked with her own veterinarian, this mistake would likely have been avoided.

If you discover after a purchase that your horse has a health issue, you need to assess your options. Can you prove that the seller or seller's veterinarian didn't disclose the health issue? Can you get your veterinarian to say that the other veterinarian should have known about the horse's health problem? This can be difficult—the veterinary industry is a small, tight-knit community, and many people may be unwilling to talk on the record about other people in their industry as they want to preserve their business relationships.

After you assess your options and how likely you are to prevail in your case, it's usually a financial decision. The legal process is expensive and time-consuming. How much did you spend on the horse? Will the amount of money you could get back be worth it? Or is it easier to just accept the loss and keep or sell the horse? Unfortunately, if you have a poorly written contract, the odds that you'll be able to have a successful lawsuit are lowered, and you may end up having to take the loss.

Flying into a Bad Purchase

A buyer, Anthony, flew out of state to try a horse named Pegasus for his young daughter, Chloe, to ride. On the first day, Chloe tried the horse, and the trial did not go well and Anthony didn't think it was a good idea to buy Pegasus. But when he went back to his hotel, he thought, "We flew across the country to see this horse, and while we are here, Chloe might as well give the horse another try tomorrow." Because he had spent the money and time to travel to see the horse, he was incentivized to buy Pegasus to make the trip worth it.

The next day, Chloe tried Pegasus again, and Pegasus was perfect. Chloe even jumped higher than she ever had before. The seller showed him show videos of Pegasus, and the horse looked great. He bought Pegasus and took her home.

After about a month, Pegasus started having behavior issues that made it dangerous for Chloe to ride. Specifically, it had a tendency to stop at jumps. Anthony decided that he didn't feel comfortable letting Chloe ride Pegasus anymore, as her safety was more important to him than anything else.

Anthony's trainer said, "Clearly, this is something Pegasus has done before. She isn't just getting spooked on occasion—She has a pattern of stopping at a jump every time. The seller would have known about this. You should try to get your money back."

Anthony went to an attorney for help returning Pegasus. The attorney asked Anthony about the trial, and he explained how the horse had behaved differently on Day 1 and Day 2. That should have been his first red flag.

With the attorney's help, Anthony realized that the show videos the seller sent were only from the second week of a two-week show. They tracked down the video from the first week, and it showed Pegasus clearly misbehaving in the same way it was now behaving with Chloe. Anthony let the costs he had incurred in flying across the country push him into having Chloe try the horse the second day, which ultimately left him with a much more expensive problem (an unsafe horse) than his and Chloe's airfare.

When a seller shows you a video of a horse...

When a seller gives you show videos, keep in mind that you're watching selective clips of the horse that may not reflect the full picture. If you're buying a horse for your child, keep in mind that your child may be much less skilled and experienced than the rider in the video. An adult rider knows how to handle the horse, but if your daughter is still learning how to ride, she may get bucked off. When this happens, you may be surprised because the horse seemed so well-behaved in the videos you saw. But the video you saw is just a snapshot of several minutes of the horse's behavior.

A $50,000 Assumption

An equestrian, Amber, was purchasing a once-in-a-lifetime horse called Atlas. She planned to use Atlas for ranch riding activities and certain types of ranch competition. Atlas was advertised as a capable horse that was perfect for ranch riding activities. The seller, Greg, specifically warranted and guaranteed that Atlas was sold with a pre-purchase exam and sold sound. Amber purchased Atlas through an auction company for $30,000.

Once the horse arrived at Amber's facility and she started riding it, she noticed that it was tripping frequently and seemed sore. Because Atlas had come through an auction company that had warranted and guaranteed potential buyers and consumers that the horse was sold with a pre-purchase exam, Amber hadn't done any additional veterinary exams. When she noticed the horse seemed sore, she asked for copies of the pre-sale X-rays, something she should have had her own vet review before the purchase. Her own vet determined that the horse suffered from navicular syndrome, which can lead to completely disabling lameness that makes a horse unable to be ridden.

When Amber and her veterinarian looked into the medical records further, they realized that Atlas had had intermittent lameness in that foot for over 3 years. Before the purchase, the auction company had Atlas do a brief lameness exam, and they determined that the horse was sound. Initially, the seller, Greg (who was separate from the auction company), said that Atlas was not lame before the sale, but he did say that Atlas had tripped frequently and that they had changed Atlas's shoes. Greg conceded that the prior X-rays had shown some irregularities, but that they were of no concern.

Amber asked for her money back, and Greg said he didn't have it anymore. Amber then contacted the auction company and was told that the company didn't research every single horse and that they could do absolutely nothing about the sale. The representative said that the company does their best to try to keep this stuff from happening but that 1 out of 68 horses wasn't bad. Initially, they said they would refund Amber's money, but that never materialized. Amber was then only left with the possibility of filing a lawsuit.

This is an example of a case where people rely on statements that are made and don't do their due diligence by getting their own veterinarian to do a pre-purchase exam or seeking out past veterinarian records before buying the horse. If Amber had followed all of those procedures before purchase, the issue could have been avoided. Now, Amber had lost close to $50,000 and had to file a lawsuit to try to recover some of that money.

Many issues can be prevented or improved with good contracts. It's crucial to consult with someone who is not financially invested in the transaction. If you've worked with an outside eye to identify red flags before a sale, it'll be easier to walk away and find a horse that won't give you any problems.

CHAPTER 4

Horse Owners - Understanding and Minimizing Your Liability Risk

If your horse hurts someone or causes property damage, you could be liable...

The horse that Lisa and John bought for their daughter Jessica is boarded at the stable where Jessica trains. One day, the horse gets spooked and kicks another young rider, breaking her arm. This rider's parents are upset and file a lawsuit against Lisa and John, who are astonished. They never considered the fact that such a situation could happen and that they could be liable for the actions of Jessica's horse... When they contact a lawyer about the situation, the lawyer asks them what horse-related insurance they have. Lisa and John look at each other in horror. "We didn't even think about that," Lisa says.

Many first-time horse owners fail to realize that they are potentially liable for injuries and damages caused by their horse. Horses are large, unpredictable animals, which is different from most other assets that people own. If you own a car, you can avoid liability by driving carefully and obeying the law. But you can't sit down with a horse and explain that it has to behave well so you don't end up in court. No matter how well-trained your horse is, one incident in which it gets spooked and acts erratically can have legal and financial consequences for you and your family. You can't stop your horse from causing these incidents, but you can protect yourself from liability before such an incident occurs.

There are two primary methods to safeguard yourself from liability: insurance and well-crafted contracts. However, before delving into the details of protection, it is crucial for you, as the horse owner, to understand the various ways through which your horse might expose you to liability.

The Types of Liability You Face

Your Horse Injures a Person

If your horse injures someone, you could be liable.

A horse owner operated a farm that sold flowers, vegetables, and other plants. They also provided horse boarding services and had a paddock for their horses near the parking lot. One day, a family brought their two-year-old son to buy vegetables. When they were walking to their car, they stopped to look at the horses. The little boy stood near the fence as his dad petted a horse. Another horse walked over, and as the dad turned to look at it, the horse he had been petting reached over the fence and bit the two-year-old's cheek, removing a large portion of his flesh. The injury required surgery and left a permanent scar. The incident resulted in a lawsuit.

In this case, the injured person was not even a rider, just a visitor to the property. The horse owners likely had never considered the possibility that the horse could injure visitors to the property in this way, so they were not prepared when the family sued.

Your Horse Damages Property

Molly went to the county fairgrounds with her family, as a horse show was happening. The family stood to watch the horse show in a grassy area near the arena. Elizabeth, the exhibitor, suddenly lost control of her horse, and the horse ran through the fence near where Molly's family was standing. The horse broke two of the three horizontal fence boards, and those boards suddenly struck Molly, knocked her to the ground, broke her left wrist, and injured her back. Molly's family ended up filing a lawsuit against the horse show management and Elizabeth's parents (the owners of the horse) because it was not a reasonable expectation that Molly would be injured as a spectator. The fairgrounds then brought a suit against Elizabeth's parents for the damage Elizabeth's horse caused to the fairgrounds.

Besides an injury to a person, horses can also cause property damage, and you, as the owner, could be liable.

When it comes to liability for your horse's actions, expect the unexpected. Your horse is a large animal with a mind of its own. Even if it's generally well-behaved, circumstances could cause it to behave erratically and hurt someone or cause damage.

Your Horse Injures Another Horse

The Grant family boards their prizewinning horse, Sunshine, at a local stable. One day, Sunshine gets spooked and kicks another horse, Butterscotch, in the leg, causing a fracture. Butterscotch's owner, Mindy, is devastated, as her horse can no longer compete this season due to the injury. She files a lawsuit against Mr. and Mrs. Grant, who are surprised. They can't control Sunshine's actions—are they really liable for the injury to this expensive horse?

While training, boarding, or attending competitions, your horse may be close to other horses. If your horse causes injury to another horse, you could be liable.

Your Horse Causes an Accident

There are often incidents where a motorist becomes injured after striking a horse that has escaped an enclosure. It's common for motorists in this situation to sue the horse owner, stating that the owner failed to secure their horse properly. In one incident, a motorist who used this reasoning successfully sued for over $800,000 in damages.

Several years ago, there was an incident in which three horses escaped a paddock and ran onto a busy highway. Several drivers hit the horses, including one driver who was a surgical cardiologist. As a result of her injuries, she would not be able to practice surgery again and sued the stable for millions of dollars to replace the income she would have earned as a surgeon for the rest of her life. The horse owner was also liable for any cars that were totaled, other drivers injured, or public property damaged as a result of the horses running onto the highway.

This was a freak accident that no one expected…yet it happened. As a horse owner, you need to prepare for any possibility so you are protected if your horse causes an accident.

Protecting Yourself From Liability

Debunking Myths About Insurance

Insurance is critical if you own horses – but having insurance in and of itself is not enough; you need to make sure you have the right type of insurance and enough coverage.

Many people believe in these three myths of insurance:

1) Myth: My homeowner's policy covers it…
2) Myth: My umbrella policy covers it…
3) Myth: My trainer has insurance; therefore, I don't need insurance…

The truth is, your homeowner's or umbrella policy will generally not protect against horse-related liability exposure. Non-horse-specific insurance agents may have no clue that your policies don't cover you because they don't deal with horses, so they don't know the risks involved.

In one instance, a family purchased a $5 million umbrella policy from a non-horse-specific insurance agent. Tragically, the horse ended up killing someone, and the family discovered that there was an exclusion in the policy, so they were not covered. The insurance agent had no idea that there was this gap in the policy because he wasn't familiar with liability related to horses. This was a devastating situation, and it could have been prevented if the family had gone to an insurance agent who specialized in horses rather than opting for a generic umbrella policy.

Trainers carry insurance that is meant to protect them and their business. In most instances, a trainer's insurance won't provide protection for a client. If your trainer doesn't have the correct worker's compensation insurance, you could be exposed. If your horse kicks your trainer's employee in the leg and your trainer doesn't have worker's compensation, the next person they'll go after is the owner—you. Horse owners usually have deeper pockets than trainers. If the horse causes damage or injury, it's usually easier and more fruitful to go after the owner than the trainer. If you don't pay attention to these details, be prepared to become a target.

Personal Horse Owner's Liability Insurance

Personal horse owner's liability insurance is relatively inexpensive and can be obtained through a specialty broker. This type of insurance typically offers protection if your horse harms a person, damages property, injures another horse, or even triggers an accident. Many insurance firms start by proposing a one-million-dollar policy, but oftentimes, clients require more coverage than this initial offering.

I frequently illustrate to my clients the dual role of insurance. Primarily, insurance serves as a financial safety net that covers the cost of a claim if you find yourself on the losing end of a lawsuit. Second, and sometimes even more crucial, it furnishes you with experienced insurance defense lawyers who will represent your interests in case of a claim. Our office recommends that anyone who owns a horse carry personal horse owner's liability insurance.

Why Well-Drafted Contracts Are Crucial

In addition to having proper insurance, investing time and resources into the creation of well-drafted legal documents is another fundamental aspect of limiting liability exposure. These documents might include purchase agreements, boarding contracts, or liability waivers that protect your interests and delineate responsibilities clearly. These are designed to mitigate the potential of legal disputes or litigation, thereby reducing your potential exposure to risk.

California is one of only two states that doesn't have an equine liability statute, but that doesn't mean that a release in California is not valid. Properly drafted release of liability documents have been enforced by the California courts.

A recent case in California confirmed that a liability waiver, signed by a parent or guardian on behalf of a minor child, stating that a trainer would not be held responsible for any potential incidents while the child was under the trainer's instruction, was legally binding.

Sadly, the case in question was tragic. It involved the death of a teenage rider, which sent her family into grief and crisis, and they naturally looked for someone to hold responsible—their daughter's trainer.

The teenager, who was an accomplished rider, participated in a three-day equestrian event. As she was competing in the cross-country portion of the competition, the horse refused to jump three times. After the third refusal, she was dismissed from the competition. Despite the disqualification, the teen rider continued on, directing her horse to attempt another jump. The horse refused again and, tragically, toppled over on her, causing fatal injuries.

The teenager's parents initiated a lawsuit against the trainer, but their case was unsuccessful. The issue debated was whether the signed release effectively blocked the lawsuit. It was found that the release was indeed binding. This case underscores the importance of having a carefully constructed release of liability document. Given the absence of an equine liability statute in California, it is incumbent upon you, the horse owner, to guarantee your protection. If someone intends to ride your horse, ensure you enlist the help of an attorney to craft a release of liability form. While it might not offer absolute protection (which is where your insurance steps in), it certainly steps up your defense and brings you closer to peace of mind.

With proper insurance and well-drafted legal documents, you will not completely eliminate your liability exposure from your horse, but you can limit it significantly to the point where owning a horse doesn't have to be a scary endeavor.

CHAPTER 5

Horse Owners - How to Avoid Surprises When You Change Trainers or Boarding Facilities

After several years with the same trainer, Jessica tells her parents that she feels like her trainer is no longer pushing her to be a better rider, and she wants to move to another trainer in town with some of her friends who have had great success. The family considers the move for a few months, and after meeting with the new trainer, they decide that this trainer's program is more compatible with Jessica's goals. They give the current trainer notice that they're leaving, and they think everything was handled smoothly. But a week later, the old trainer hands them a pile of bills. "You can't leave until you pay these bills you owe me." John and Lisa are confused. They thought they had been up to date with their payments. They don't want to enter a stressful dispute with this trainer, but they don't know where these bills are coming from and don't want to be overcharged... How will they settle this?

90% of horse owners are going to change trainers or facilities at some point.

The unspoken challenge of leaving a trainer or training facility is that it can be like leaving a family. It isn't as simple as moving from one apartment to another. You have relationships with the trainer, the owner of the facility, and the community of people who board their horses there.

The facility will lose revenue, and the trainer will lose a client, which can be upsetting. If a family has multiple horses, this move can be a large financial hit to the trainer and boarding facility, which may cause conflict.

Sometimes, a horse owner has made the mistake of entering a co-ownership agreement with a trainer, and this can complicate the end of the relationship even further, especially if there is no exit plan in the co-ownership agreement or worse, no written agreement at all.

Are We Partners?

Jane purchased two stallions and hired Terry, a trainer, to ride and manage their breeding. There was no written contract between Jane and Terry. Things went well for several years, but after a certain point, Jane felt that Terry was mismanaging the horses and wanted to move them. Terry had built her whole business around these two stallions and claimed that she and Jane had entered into an oral partnership agreement and that she actually owned 25% of these two horses, and therefore, Jane could not move the horses. Subsequently, an expensive and time-consuming lawsuit evolved. Both parties could have avoided this lawsuit by either not entering a co-ownership agreement in the first place (these agreements usually end in disputes) or by having a well-drafted contract with an exit plan.

When a horse owner leaves a trainer, there can be a lot of emotion involved, and if there are legal issues, tensions can run high. In the same way, sometimes it might be a trainer who needs to ask a horse owner to leave their program. Terminating these relationships, whether you are the horse owner or the trainer, needs to be done in a deliberate, carefully considered way.

To successfully prepare for a smooth transition to a new trainer or facility, ensure that you have a reliable place to move to, that you have all your invoices, and that they are paid in full. A constant problem with boarding facilities and trainers is that often they do not bill regularly. This presents a major problem for all parties: the boarding facility, the trainers, and the boarders. If a boarder is leaving, there will likely be billing disputes. These disputes can be avoided if all parties discuss billing before the boarder leaves. If you're the boarder, it's in your best interest to ensure you've paid everything you owe the trainer and facility before giving your notice.

Over the years, I've seen many instances where horse owners leaving a facility are suddenly presented with thousands of dollars worth of bills that the trainer claims haven't been paid. They give their notice, and the next thing they know, they're hit with a pile of bills that they don't think they should owe. I've seen these unexpected bills range from $15,000 to six figures.

I've personally been through multiple situations where I've gone with a client to transfer the horses, the trainer demands payments and won't tell us how much it is, and the client and

I stand there with a check waiting to pay it off, only to be met with more and more demands.

Some of you may be thinking, "If a trainer does this to me, why couldn't I just take them to court?" You could take them to court, but that process could take a year or longer... And that could be a year without your horses, and often, the legal fees you would pay to bring that lawsuit don't make it economically feasible.

If this billing situation happens to you, the most likely solution is that you and your attorney will have to negotiate to get your horse back--and you may end up having to pay the trainer or boarding facility to get your horse back, even if you know that you don't owe the amount they claim you owe.

From the boarding stable or trainer's perspective, they might need to ask a horse owner to leave their training program, and when they ask them to leave, the horse owner refuses to pay any further training bills. This can be a financial hardship for the trainer. To prevent this, ensure that everything is up to date, check that you don't have any outstanding bills, and then give your notice.

A Checklist for Moving to a New Barn

Transitioning to a new trainer or facility or asking someone to leave your training program can be a complex task, and it can potentially be a source of stress. A thorough, organized, and efficient approach can go a long way toward ensuring the process is smooth and effective. Below is a checklist of things to consider before you decide to move barns.

☑ Research and Selection. Before even thinking about making a move, take the time to extensively research potential new trainers or facilities. Consider their reputations, offerings, costs, locations, and any other factors that are important to you. You might also want to visit these locations or talk with the trainers to get a feel for their styles and expectations. Choosing a reliable and suitable place is the first step to a successful transition.

☑ Review Your Current Contract. It's essential to review your current contract to understand the terms and conditions related to termination or transfer. Some facilities or trainers may require a notice period, while others may impose fees for early termination.

☑ Invoices and Payments. Ensure that you are fully paid up at your current facility. Double-check all invoices, make sure there are no outstanding payments, and clear any pending amounts. This not only prevents any potential issues or disputes down the line but also ensures you leave on a good note.

☑ Communication. Once you have decided on a new trainer or facility, keep open lines of communication. Inform your current facility about your decision to move. Provide the current facility with written notice that you are giving your thirty-day (or whatever time your contract requires) notice. Moreover, communicate with your new trainer or facility about your plans, expectations, and any concerns you might have.

☑ Information Transfer. To provide continuity for your horse, make sure the new stable and trainer have all the necessary information about you and your horse. This could include your training history, your horse's vet history, including vaccinations, when your horse was last shod, and any dietary issues your horse might have. This will help your new stable and trainer get up to speed on you and your horse and build upon your previous training progress instead of starting from scratch.

☑ Transition Plan. Develop a transition plan that covers when and how you'll make the move. Who will trailer your horse to the new facility? Will your new trainer make those arrangements for you, or do you need to make them? Who will be at the barn to receive your horse? Depending on your situation, you might need to wind down activities at your current facility while ramping up at the new one. A clear timeline and sequence of activities can help make this process smoother.

☑ Integration. Once you've made the move, take the time to get acquainted with the new environment. Learn about the facility's rules, culture, and expectations. Try to develop a good working relationship with your new trainer and any other key individuals.

☑ Regular Assessment. As you settle into your new barn, regularly assess your progress and satisfaction. If there are areas where your expectations aren't being met, don't hesitate to bring them up with your new trainer or barn manager. The goal of the transition is not just to change locations or trainers but to find a place where you can continue to grow and excel.

By following these steps, you can navigate the transition to a new trainer or facility with confidence and clarity. It might require effort and patience, but the potential benefits in terms of your training can make it well worth it.

What to Know About the Agister's Lien

The Agister's Lien (California Civil Code section §3080) is one of the oldest laws in California. This law allows a boarding operator to put a lien on a horse if the horse owner hasn't paid for the horse's food, water, and shelter. To perfect the lien, you have to go to court and file a lawsuit, which is expensive.

Sometimes, when there is conflict about an owner leaving a trainer or facility, the trainer or facility can use this lien against the owner and hold custody of the horse until they're paid.

However, many people mistakenly believe this lien applies to training fees, it doesn't. The purpose of the lien is to protect animals by ensuring that owners provide for the horse's basic needs. Under the Agister's Lien, a trainer cannot hold custody of the horse due to unpaid training fees.

It's important to know that the Agister's Lien does not apply to training fees in case you encounter a trainer who claims you owe training bills and tries to keep possession of your horse under lien laws. Many times, trainers don't know that the Agister's Lien does not apply to training fees, so they may simply be mistaken and believe they are within their legal rights to hold your horse until you pay them what they believe you owe.

CHAPTER 6

Violations of Rules of the Sport

When you attend events sanctioned by the United States Equestrian Federation (USEF) or Fédération Équestre Internationale (FEI), there's a possibility that you could be accused of violating the rules of the sport. If this happens, you'll get a letter informing you of the violation. It may be a surprise to you.

Many people who get these letters aren't trying to break the rules. The rules of the sport are complicated, and they may change every year. For example, in certain international competitions for jumpers, the type of boots that horses wear are regulated, and this rule may change slightly from year to year. USEF and FEI rules are also different from each other, and there's a lot you could miss if you aren't paying close attention.

Horse owners are busy people. You likely aren't sitting down to read the rulebook each year as it's updated. It's not uncommon for owners to make innocent mistakes because they weren't informed. It's crucial to work with a trainer who has a familiarity with the rules and is committed to helping you and your horse stay in compliance.

If you are accused of violating a rule, the consequences can range from warnings to fines to suspensions, which could be months, years, or even indefinite suspension.

When you're suspended, you cannot compete. This can have devastating consequences for both you and your trainer, who makes a living from training and competing in horse shows. If they're banned from the sport for even a month, it can be a huge loss of income.

There is also not much room for negotiation regarding the time of your suspension. If you're suspended for one month, and the month selected by the USEF happens to be a month that you have an important competition, there is little you can do to change that. You would be forced to miss the competition and lose that opportunity.

There are two common types of rule violations: medication-related violations and sportsmanship violations.

At horse shows, horses are subjected to random drug tests. These samples are analyzed for violations, and it can be a lengthy process. If you're accused of a medication violation, you may not be notified until months later. If you get a letter claiming that your horse had banned substances in its system, you have a certain number of days to request that the "B" sample be tested or to request a hearing.

If you request a hearing, you will likely have to go to a USEF hearing in Kentucky, where you will present your evidence to a committee of three people. USEF will have its representative present to argue why it is a violation. You can have your attorney present your case as to why there was no violation. As mentioned below, I strongly recommend you contact an equine attorney who is experienced in this area if you receive a rule violation. Following the hearing, the committee will either rule in favor of or against you and determine a penalty.

Some horse owners may not have even known that the medication they used for their horse was against the rules. Other unintentional mistakes are possible—for example, some common medications or ointments are permitted, but an amount above a certain dosage could be flagged as a positive drug test. There are some medications that come as a cream. The rules only allow owners to administer two inches of this cream to be applied to the horse's body. Due to the way this medication is applied, it can be easy to accidentally apply more than 2 inches of the cream. You're likely not measuring this paste with a ruler... and if the cream was applied to an area on the horse that was clipped, it might absorb quicker than if it was applied to an unclipped area, potentially causing a rule violation.

Other unintentional mistakes are possible. Some rules permit certain medications, but only if they're taken a certain number of days before competing. A horse is a living creature, and each horse may process medication slightly differently. If there are trace elements of medication still in your horse's system, you could face consequences for an innocent mistake.

When thinking about sportsmanship rules, it's important to remember that once you step onto the horse show grounds as a competitor, trainer, or exhibitor, the organization has jurisdiction over your conduct there. Behaviors that may not seem "illegal" or that occur in the heat of the moment may get you into trouble, even if you aren't expecting it.

How to Respond to a Rules Violation

The good news is that being accused of a rule violation is not the end of the world. There are concrete actions you can take to challenge the accusation and prevent penalties.

The moment you receive a rule violation letter, you should contact an attorney. It's crucial that you don't bury your head in the sand and hope the problem will go away on its own if you ignore it. You need to be proactive and take steps to deal with the problem.

Many of the actions you can take are time-sensitive, so the sooner you contact an attorney, the more options you'll have. But if you wait until the day before the deadline to contact an attorney, there may not be much you can do to fight the accusation.

After you contact an attorney, you should make a copy of the letter for your attorney and begin the process of collecting the facts. Contact any trainers, grooms, or other witnesses who were present when the rule was allegedly violated and try to get a written statement from them.

When you have the facts, you and your attorney can assess your options. If you can prove your innocence, you may opt for a hearing, but you may decide that the proposed penalty is preferable to the time and expense involved in a hearing to challenge the accusation. For example, if your penalty will be a small fine, and the attorney and travel fees associated with proving your innocence total more than the fine, you may decide to resolve the problem by simply paying the fine. Expenses for a hearing can range anywhere from $15,000-$30,000.

You'll need to pay attorney fees for your attorney to prepare for the hearing and prepare to respond to the other side's evidence. The hearing is like a mini-court trial, so these fees can be costly. Also, keep in mind that you'll often have to pay for your attorney to travel to Kentucky.

A Word About Safe Sport Rules

The Safe Sport rules cover all Olympic sports. Anyone over 18 must go through Safe Sport abuse awareness and prevention training every year to be a member of USEF.

If you or your employee are ever on the wrong end of a Safe Sport complaint, you should contact your attorney immediately and not talk to anyone about the complaint.

It's important to note that Safe Sport complaints can be made anonymously to protect the victim. If there's an alleged Safe Sport violation, the investigation goes out of the hands of USEF.

There are certain Safe Sport rules you may not even realize you're breaking. For example, Safe Sport bans adults from texting minors without another adult present in the chat. What happens if an innocent mistake such as texting a minor about their competition time leads to an accusation?

If this occurs, it's crucial to get advice from an attorney. Again, if you take the time to familiarize yourself with these rules, you can avoid situations that could lead to violations.

CHAPTER 7

Horse Property Owners - Liability Risk and Safeguarding Your Investment

Now that Jessica is a committed equestrian, her parents are spending large sums of money each year on boarding at the local stable. But more importantly, they've fallen in love with the horse owner's life. John begins daydreaming about owning a large, beautiful property with a stable in the back. He could save money on his daughter's boarding costs and also enjoy a tranquil lifestyle, sitting on the porch with his wife and watching their daughter ride. He gets his family on board with the idea. When they find a property they like, they purchase it. Time for the good life to begin, right? Not so much...

When you own a horse property, there are a myriad of situations that could put you at risk for liability—and Lisa and John haven't taken time to think through these possible situations and protect their new asset.

What if their new property isn't zoned for agriculture? What if Jessica brings friends over, and the horse bites one of them? What if the horse gets loose and causes damage to a neighbor's car?

If you're like many horse property owners, you think, "It can't happen to me"... And this mindset puts you completely at risk because you haven't protected yourself from potential liability.

Often, people buy horse properties without any experience with horses. Others have been around horses but never considered the risk and liability of owning a horse property. People get enamored with the romantic idea of having horses on the property and fail to consider the necessity of protecting their property from liability.

Sometimes, a realtor tells a prospective property owner, "You can run a horse stable and have a passive stream of income!" and they get excited. But having live animals on your property is riskier than other popular passive income streams like running an Airbnb... You need to be sure you know what you're getting into.

You may not realize that you're putting your property, livelihood, and wealth at risk. And if you live on the property, you could be putting your family's home at risk without even knowing it. These risks are present even if you only have your horses on the property or only deal with your friends. For example, Priscilla owned a horse property for over thirty years and only boarded her friends' horses on her property. She never carried proper insurance because it was too expensive, and she figured she would be fine because she was careful about whom she let keep their horses on her property. One of her boarders brought a friend over to the barn, and that friend slipped on some hay in the barn aisle and fell but, to Priscilla's relief, walked away with no apparent injuries. A few months later, Priscilla was slapped with a lawsuit for the visitor's claims of back injuries. She didn't have insurance to step up and provide her with a defense or help pay settlement costs. After thirty years of living in the same place, she was facing losing her home.

A real estate agent may not warn you about these risks. It's not very enticing to tell a potential buyer, "This $4 million property is gorgeous, but if someone falls off a horse and gets killed, you could be looking at the other end of a wrongful death lawsuit." A real estate agent will usually only say things that will help them sell the property because that's their job...but it means that you could be sold a beautiful, million-dollar property without getting a heads-up about how to prepare for the risks and protect your new asset.

I recommend that everyone looking to buy a horse property consult with an equine attorney before closing a deal so you're fully aware of any liabilities you could be getting into before you make a final decision. If you do purchase the property, this also allows you to prepare for any potential risks ahead of time.

If owning a horse property is your dream, you can do it responsibly—as long as you understand the risks and mitigate them.

With horses, you're dealing with a large animal that has a mind of its own and may react in a way you don't expect. There is always the possibility that an accident could occur. An attorney can help with risk management by minimizing your risk of a lawsuit or financial consequences.

Some clients, after talking with an attorney, decide the risk of owning a horse property isn't worth it to them. I believe that if owning a horse property is your dream, you can do it responsibly—as long as you understand the risks and mitigate them.

To mitigate these risks, you need the 3-legged stool of protection.

Each leg represents one way you protect your liability. The three legs together hold the stool up, and those legs are appropriate insurance, proper release forms, and incorporation.

Appropriate Insurance

Making sure you, as the property owner, have the right type of coverage and enough coverage are the two most important things you can do to protect yourself when the worst-case scenario happens. Insurance not only provides you protection for a payout, but if there is a lawsuit, it will also provide you with a set of insurance defense attorneys to represent you and the insurance company's interests in the case.

Depending on what part of the horse industry your business focuses on, there are different types of insurance which I will go into in more detail at the end of this chapter.

Proper Release of Liability Forms

The second leg of the stool is a well-drafted Release of Liability/ Assumption of Risk Waiver.

Forty-eight states have what is known as an Equine Liability Statute, but California and Maryland do not. Some people erroneously think that means that there is no liability protection in the horse industry in those two states. You've probably heard someone say, "That release form isn't worth the paper it's written on," but that is not true. Not having an equine liability statute means that attorneys have to keep up with case law to see what the courts want in a release to make it valid.

Incorporation

Having a properly incorporated business, whether it is an S-Corp, a C-Corp, or an LLC gives you an added layer of protection and is the third leg of the stool. In a perfect world, when someone is injured, they would file a lawsuit against this corporation, and your personal assets would be protected. However, as you know, we don't live in a perfect world. In our experience, having handled multiple lawsuits, even with a corporation, the individual is almost always named as well. Now, the majority of lawsuits settle before a trial, so this issue is not often adjudicated. However, I never want someone to leave a conversation thinking that by having a corporation, they have a silver bullet to protect their liability. Incorporating is another layer of protection between your horse property and a lawsuit.

If you are like many of our clients, you are excellent at what it is that you offer to your customers, but more likely than not, you don't know all the risks that are lurking in your business.

Like a three-legged stool, your protection measures won't stand up without all three legs. For example, if you have insurance and contracts, but you don't have an ownership entity, you won't be fully protected.

What are the risks of owning a horse property?

The two major categories of liability are injury to a person and injury to a horse.

Injuries to a Person

A person getting injured on your horse property is your biggest area of liability exposure. It can occur with riders, spectators, volunteers, and employees and range from a minor broken bone to death.

Certain business practices can increase the risk of injury to a person on your property. If you don't require riders to wear helmets, you greatly increase the potential for injury. It is well-documented that wearing helmets saves lives, and it's such an unnecessary risk to not require it.

If your business involves working with non-riders, including trail-riding businesses or horse birthday party venues, you are also increasing risk of injury. Non-riders don't know how to handle horses, so there is a greater potential that something could go wrong. You're relying on the fact that your horse is well-behaved and that something out of control doesn't happen to spook the horse. Frequent riders know that falling off when you ride is part of learning to ride, but inexperienced riders who may be riding a horse one time for a party aren't expecting to fall, so they are more likely to be injured.

Even if guests do not ride the horses, having them present on the property is risky. For example, if you rent the property through Airbnb or a similar short-term rental service and your guests wander over to look at the stables and get kicked by a horse, you could be liable even though you didn't plan on these people interacting with your horses.

Risk of injury is present even if you only have your own horses on the property and don't run a business. Often, horse property owners will have friends over and let them ride the horse for fun. "These are just friends, not clients," they think, "since I'm not getting paid for it, there shouldn't be a problem." But if an injury or death occurs, the property owner would likely be liable and could even lose the property.

There may be circumstances you could never predict...

One night, during a terrible storm, two horses got spooked by thunder and escaped the fenced paddock of a horse property through a broken area of the fence. This property was adjacent to a busy highway. The horses ran onto the highway, causing chaos. Drivers, already having difficulty driving in heavy rain, now had to swerve to avoid the horses. Unfortunately, multiple accidents occurred. The owners of the horse property were now liable for injuries and automobile damage for anyone involved in the incident... All because they failed to properly secure a broken fence on their property.

You may have known that someone falling off a horse or getting kicked was in the realm of possibilities, but there is a whole world of possible circumstances you likely haven't thought about or prepared for.

Injuries to a Horse

With an injury to a horse, many injuries that lead to liability are random occurrences. For example, a six-figure horse was living at a boarding stable, and a fencing panel dislodged and fell on the horse, injuring it to the extent that it was never able to be ridden again. You've likely never thought about the possibility that something like that could occur. But this random, freak accident caused the horse property owner significant financial strain. Had they had better insurance and documentation, they would have been in a much better position.

Horse property owners also need to be aware of zoning liability. You may be zoned for a residential or agricultural property, but not for commercial activity. If you perform commercial services such as boarding, lessons, or parties, you may be violating zoning laws without realizing it. Under zoning laws, there may also be a limit to the number of horses you can have per acre. This could impact the profitability of your business if you can't reach full boarding capacity.

Under the Williamson Act in California, some property owners can get a reduced property tax rate because the land is dedicated to agriculture. However, the Williamson Act may not always apply to commercial horseboarding facilities. I've worked with property owners who took advice from well-intentioned real estate agents who promoted the tax savings available for agricultural land. Unless the property owners do further investigation, they may run into trouble. Yes, agricultural land may qualify for tax savings, but some subtleties in the Williamson Act exclude certain commercial horse properties from those same savings. It's best to get the opinion of an equine attorney if the tax savings are critical to your financial model for the property.

Why Insurance is Essential

To mitigate your risk, you need insurance. But insurance is not the place to save money. Invest your money in insurance to save yourself the much higher sums of money you will be liable for if an incident occurs.

Horse property owners should have:

1. **A Farm and Ranch Policy.** This is the equivalent of a homeowner's policy for your horse property. It is a highly customized policy that starts with basic coverage, and then you can add on options based on your activities on the property. You should have enough to cover replacement costs for structures on your property.

2. **A Farm Liability Policy.** A farm liability policy protects the horse property owner from legal liability if a third party, such as a visitor, gets injured on the property or if the farm's operations cause damage to another person's property. This might include instances where a horse escapes and causes damage or injury. This will also protect against personal injury claims if someone is riding on your property and falls off and is injured.

Many policies start at one million dollars in coverage, but that just doesn't cut it these days. If you are involved in a case where a minor sadly loses their life, that life will be valued at more than a million dollars. We generally recommend our clients carry a minimum of three to five million dollars in liability coverage, but of course, everyone's situation is different, which is why it is important to have a conversation with your agent about coverage.

3. A Care, Custody, and Control Policy. This is a specialized coverage that protects you if a horse under your care (but not owned by you) is injured or dies. You should have enough insurance to cover the average value of the horses on your property. You risk a lawsuit if you board high-value horses on your property but only have a small amount of insurance coverage. If a $100,000 horse is injured and the owner believes you were at fault, they won't be content with $10,000 in insurance compensation.

Myths People Believe About Insurance and Horse Properties

1) My homeowner insurance covers me.

2) My umbrella policy covers me.

3) My farm policy covers everything.

4) I have the right kind of equestrian insurance, so I'm covered.

Homeowner's insurance and umbrella policies usually don't cover certain horse-specific liabilities. Even if you do have the correct policy, it's likely that you may not have enough coverage. You may only be covered up to a certain point and could still be liable. Reviewing your insurance policies and truly understanding them is an important way to protect your horse property.

CHAPTER 8

Horse Property Owners - The Three Essential Contracts You Need

Insurance is only one piece of the puzzle when it comes to protecting yourself from liability as a horse property owner. Well-drafted contracts are necessary safeguards.

An effective contract:

1) Transfers risk
2) Limits scope
3) Limits the amount of liability

What contracts do I need?

The most important contracts horse property owners need are:

1. **Release of Liability/Assumption of Risk Agreement**
   While forty-eight states across the United States possess what's commonly referred to as an Equine Liability Statute, California and Maryland do not. This lack of a statute, however, has given rise to a common misconception that there is not as much liability protection present for the horse industry in these states. You may have even heard someone

dismissively remark, "That release form isn't worth the paper it's written on." Contrary to this belief, the absence of an equine liability statute does not equate to a total absence of liability protection.

In place of an overarching statute, California relies heavily on case law to determine liability issues in the horse industry. The case law points toward making releases understandable by a layperson, which makes sense when you consider that someone is potentially releasing away their right to bring a lawsuit if they are injured. Your release of liability should be specifically tailored to the activities that will occur on your property. A generic, off-the-shelf release you purchase from the internet might not offer you adequate protection. We have had clients come to us after there has been an accident on their property, and when we look at their release, it was drafted for a different state, and the provisions do not apply in California.

But even the best-drafted release doesn't provide 100% protection, which is why you need insurance, too. Together, insurance and a well-drafted release of liability document form a robust line of defense to protect you and your horse property.

2. Boarding Contract

A boarding contract is your opportunity to eliminate many problems before they happen and to set clear expectations so you have happy boarders and less drama at your barn. Below are some of the key provisions you should consider including in your boarding contract.

What Services Will Your Barn Provide?

- How often, how much, and what type of feed will the horses be fed?
- How often with the stalls be mucked out?
- When will the arena be dragged?
- Will your barn employees put on and take off blankets, or is that the horse owner's responsibility?
- If specific services are not specified, it can lead to disputes between you as the stable owner and the boarder.

Feeding Dispute

One recent dispute we handled was related to the amount of hay the horses were to be fed. When George purchased his horse property and decided to have boarders, he spent considerable time researching how much hay to feed the horses and how often to feed it. He settled on feeding hay three times per day and giving each horse two flakes of hay per feeding. He based his budget and financial calculations on this scenario.

Emma brought her tall, lanky thoroughbred, who had always been a hard keeper, to live at George's barn, and within a few weeks, she felt he was losing weight. Emma approached George and told him that her horse needed four flakes of hay three times per day. George was put in a hard position because his boarding contract didn't specify how much or how often the horses would be fed.

If he had specified those amounts in the boarding contract, he could have also included that extra feed was available for an additional cost. Having a detailed boarding contract and communicating those details to your clients will ensure that everyone is on the same page before a dispute about a horse's care arises.

Description of the Horse. The boarding contract should include a detailed description of the horse, including name, breed, age, color, and any distinguishing marks. Additionally, the value of the horse and whether or not the horse is insured should be included.

Payment Terms. Details of the cost of the boarding services, the method of payment, and the payment schedule should be clearly laid out. You should also include late fees if board is not paid in a timely fashion and whether or not a security deposit will be included.

Veterinary Care. This section should address health-related issues, such as vaccination requirements, routine and emergency veterinary care, and who is responsible for these costs. This should also give you, as the horse property owner, the ability to contact a veterinarian on behalf of the owner if you can't reach the owner within a certain amount of time.

Termination of the Boarding Contract. Most boarding contracts state that the boarder must provide thirty days' notice to terminate the agreement and move their horse. A well-drafted boarding contract should also include that the stable owner can terminate a contract (usually with 48 hours notice) if the boarder breaks a rule or if the horse presents a danger to a person or to the facility itself.

Without this clause, if the boarder or horse presents a danger to the facility and you give them the typical thirty days' notice, the horse will remain on the property for that amount of time, which could increase the odds that the horse will endanger other horses or boarders.

Checklist for Removing a Client (for Trainers or Stable Managers)

☑ Review your contract. Hopefully, you have a training or boarding contract with your client that specifies how much notice you have to give to ask someone to leave. If you don't, you need to get one of those drafted post haste.

☑ Invoices and Payments. Review if the client you are asking to leave owes you any money. If they do, ask for it to be paid BEFORE you ask them to leave. In my experience, the chances of getting paid as a stable or trainer once you have asked someone to leave are very low.

What to Do When a Boarder Won't Leave

If you board horses, you may find that it is time to ask a boarder to leave your facility, yet they resist. Their reasons could range from difficulty finding another suitable boarding location to simply being unwilling to move.

To protect yourself, and to minimize any conflict your boarding or training agreement should include an exit protocol.

Venue Provisions. The contract should specify the state and county to which the contract applies.

Alternative Dispute Resolution. We strongly encourage you, as the horse property owner, to include alternative dispute resolution provisions, such as mediation or arbitration, in your boarding contract. Many times litigating a dispute with a boarder does not make financial sense due to the high costs of bringing a lawsuit. By requiring mediation before the filing of a lawsuit, you have given yourself a mechanism that can save you time, money, and the stress of a lawsuit.

The Agister's Lien

The Agister's Lien (California Civil Code §3080) allows a boarding operator to put a lien on a horse if the horse owner hasn't paid for the horse's food, water, and shelter. To perfect the lien and sell the horse, the holder of the lien has to go to court and file a lawsuit. It is often advantageous to draft around the Agister's Lien, so that you, as the property owner, can sell the horse for the past due board if the board has not been paid in a certain number of days, however to do this you have to have specific language in your contract.

A Cautionary Tale

Harriet was the owner of three horses, all past their prime but still in good health. The horses were named Chance, Daisy, and Willow. Harriet had loved these horses in their prime, but as they got older and she got busier, she retired them to a stable in the country that was owned by Martha. Martha took excellent care of all the horses, ensuring they were well-fed, healthy, and comfortable in their retirement. Harriet often paid her board bill late, but Martha, empathetic towards Harriet's chaotic city life, never complained.

As the months rolled on, Harriet's visits became infrequent and then eventually ceased altogether. Harriet's board payments that were once tardy now became sparse, then stopped. Martha tried to contact Harriet through phone calls and text messages, but all her attempts echoed in a void of silence.

Four months passed without a single penny from Harriet. The stable was not affluent, and the expenses of caring for the three horses were mounting. Martha was in a difficult position; she loved Chance, Daisy, and Willow but couldn't afford to keep them any longer without payment. The problem was that Chance, Daisy, and Willow had very little re-sale value at this point due to their age. She had hoped to use the Agister's Lien to be able to sell the horses and get them off her monthly expense bill, but after talking to an attorney found out that it would cost her much more than these horses were worth to file the lawsuit and get a court order allowing her to sell the horses.

This is a story we have heard hundreds of times over the last two decades practicing equine law, and it illustrates why having a well-drafted boarding agreement that addresses this type of situation upfront is so important.

3. **Contract Between Boarding Facility and Trainer**

   A trainer's agreement is an agreement a horse property owner has with any trainer who runs a training business on your property. A trainer's agreement is even more crucial if you have multiple trainers on the property because many conflicts can arise.

   For example, what happens if two trainers want to use a certain arena at the same time? Many facilities only have one covered arena, so in the winter, there can be disputes about who gets to use it and when. If this is the case, the trainers will be making less income in the winter due to having to share this covered arena and reduce their training hours, so tensions can run high over this issue. By including this information in the contract, you can set clear expectations with each trainer in advance.

   While not exhaustive, below are some key provisions every horse property owner should have in their agreement with a resident trainer.

Key Provisions for Contracts Between Boarding Facilities and Trainers:

Use Fee. Your agreement should include what the use fee will be for the trainer. Sometimes this is commission-based, i.e. a certain percent of the trainer's gross receipts. Other times, the use fee is a flat fee.

Term and Termination. As with your boarding agreement, you will want to include how both you and the trainer can terminate the agreement. It is very important to ensure that the termination clauses in your boarding agreement and the termination clause in your agreement with the trainer are similar and include the same number of days to terminate. This is a common mistake we see when we are reviewing clients' documents during our equine business audits.

When Training Agreements and Boarding Agreements Are Not Aligned

Pete's training agreement with Flying Farms stated that he needed to give sixty days' notice to terminate. All of Pete's students had signed a boarding agreement with Flying Farms that stated they needed to give thirty days' notice to terminate. Additionally, Pete had three horses of his own, and he had signed boarding agreements for the three horses that required he give thirty-days notice to terminate.

As you can imagine, confusion arose over which contract's notice period should be followed. This led to disagreements between the barn, Pete, and his students, which then escalated into a larger dispute.

Had both the training and boarding contracts had the same notice period for termination, potential conflicts like these could have been avoided.

Trainers, Employees, and Worker's Compensation. Your agreement should specify that a trainer is responsible and agrees to properly classify their employees and to carry worker's compensation insurance.

Insurance. Your agreement should require that a trainer carry professional liability insurance and that you, as the property owner, are listed as an additional insured. This will protect you if one of their students is injured and brings a lawsuit.

Indemnification. In addition to insurance, the training agreement should include an indemnification clause stating that the trainer indemnifies you, the property owner, against any loss that occurs on the property during their use.

Use of Property. Your agreement should specify what parts of the property the trainer has exclusive use of and what parts of the property are shared use.

Creating a detailed agreement with the trainer operating on your premises can play a critical role in establishing transparency and setting mutual expectations. This foundational document outlines the rights and responsibilities of both parties, which helps prevent potential misunderstandings and disagreements.

For you, as the horse property owner, this agreement becomes a tool to maintain harmony on your premises, ensuring that the activities carried out by the trainer align with your property's rules and values. This alignment not only contributes to the preservation of your property but also enhances the reputation and appeal of your facility among horse owners and trainers alike.

A Note on Purchasing a Horse Property - Zoning

Before you purchase a horse property, in addition to performing the normal due diligence involved in purchasing a property, you should also consult with an equine attorney.

You cannot assume that the current owner has complied with local zoning laws. Zoning rules change from county to county, and often a county does not enforce them until there is a complaint. You don't want to purchase your dream horse property and then discover that it cannot be used for the purpose you intended...

Zoning rules are often much more stringent for commercial horse properties than they are for residential horse properties – this means if you are buying a property that has been used only for one family's horses and you are planning to run a business on it, you might be violating your county's zoning rules. Consulting with an equine attorney can help you ensure your use of the property will comply with the law before you purchase it.

CHAPTER 9

Horse Property Owners - Navigating Employment Law Risk

Do you have employees? You might be surprised to find out that the answer is yes.

If anyone works on your property, you might have employment law issues…even if you think they are your trainer's employee. If your trainer has employees on the property, they may be classified as your employees, and you don't even know it. This can even occur if you hire a business to do work on your property.

Fred, a horse property owner, hired a local business, The Fence Master, to fix a portion of his fence. The Fence Master sent its workers to Fred's property, and in the process of fixing the fence, one of these workers allegedly was injured. As it turned out, The Fence Master was unlicensed and did not have worker's compensation insurance, so Fred was held responsible for hiring an unlicensed worker, even though he had no idea The Fence Master was unlicensed. He had chosen them because they gave him the lowest bid. If you hire an outside company to work on your property, even if they aren't working with horses, ensure that they're properly licensed so you won't be held responsible for a worker's injuries.

Navigating the complexities of employee classification can be challenging, particularly due to the differing criteria outlined by the Internal Revenue Service (IRS) and the Department of Labor (DOL). While each serves its purpose, these standards can create potential difficulties and liabilities for businesses if they aren't closely adhered to.

Misclassification of your employees can have significant consequences. From a financial perspective, the IRS may hold you responsible for back taxes and penalties for not withholding and paying income taxes, Social Security, Medicare, and unemployment taxes on wages paid to misclassified workers.

The implications don't end there - errors in classification can also lead to complications with worker's compensation insurance, potentially leaving your business exposed to severe financial risks. However, the impacts of misclassification are not solely financial. The strain on your business operations and reputation can also be damaging. The DOL is particularly vigilant regarding employee rights and fair labor standards. Knowingly misclassifying your workers can lead to civil and criminal penalties. These penalties can be substantial, crippling your business operations and tarnishing your reputation.

Correct classification of employees is not just a legal requirement but also crucial for maintaining your business's stability, integrity, and long-term viability. Understanding and adhering to the standards set forth by the IRS and the DOL is imperative so that you don't put your biggest investment – your horse property – at risk.

Many horse property owners do not initially start their journey into the horse industry as business owners. They didn't necessarily go into purchasing the property with a business plan or understanding the legal requirements of running a business; instead, they might have purchased their property to keep their children's ponies on, and over the years, a full horse operation evolved, this is why having a trusted attorney advisor can be invaluable.

Navigating Employee Injuries

If a worker is injured on the job, the repercussions can multiply, especially if that worker has been misclassified. Misclassification may leave you liable for medical expenses, compensation claims, and potential lawsuits. Not only can this lead to financial consequences, but it could also result in operational disruptions and potentially long-lasting damage to your business and its reputation. **If someone working on your property gets injured, you should immediately contact your attorney.**

Often, property owners will think, "My employee is going to the emergency room. I will do the decent thing and pay his hospital bills." However, this may not be the best thing to do from a legal perspective. If there's a full investigation, this action could imply that you were liable for the injury, and you could get into more trouble or owe more money.

It's the human impulse to want to care for your employee, but you should call your attorney before doing so to ensure any action you take won't hurt you in the long run. There are other ways to support your employee after an injury that won't cause legal issues later. Your attorney will be able to advise you on the best way to proceed.

Compliance with Minimum Wage and other Employment Laws

Every state has different minimum wage laws. As a horse property owner, you must ensure you comply with minimum wage laws for any employees on your property. This also includes giving employees the proper amount of time for breaks. Traditionally, stables that employ grooms have had them work long hours due to the nature of the business. It is not unusual for a groom's day to start with the sun rising and finish when the sun is setting, but that approach is no longer viable in today's legal climate. It is imperative as a horse property owner that you educate yourself on the relevant employment laws and create systems and processes so that your employees can follow them.

Retaining the Previous Owner's Employees

Many times we see new horse property owners purchase a horse property that already has a workforce in place. It's not uncommon for our clients to choose to continue employing these individuals. The underlying rationale is that these workers have valuable experience and familiarity with the property. For instance, they might know how to use specific equipment that comes with the purchase or perhaps what areas of the property might be at risk of flooding in extreme weather. The common mistake many new owners make is taking for granted that the preceding owner has appropriately managed all employment-related concerns. Unfortunately, this isn't always the case. It's possible that certain issues were overlooked or mismanaged by the previous owner, which could lead to potential legal complications or employee dissatisfaction down the line.

As a new property owner, conducting a comprehensive review of all employment matters is critical to ensure everything is in order before making the purchase, particularly if you plan to rely on these employees from day one. Not only will this prevent potential future disputes, but it also ensures a smooth transition and provides a more secure and pleasant working environment for the staff.

While this chapter offers a high-level overview of potential employment issues for horse property owners to be aware of, it doesn't come close to encompassing every possible scenario. If you employ individuals on your horse property and have yet to consult with an attorney, it's critical that you seek legal advice immediately. Without a thorough understanding of the laws and regulations, you may unintentionally expose your investment to unnecessary risks.

CHAPTER 10

Empowering Trainers - Strategies for Protecting Yourself and Your Clients

Robert is a successful trainer, but he does things "the way they've always been done"–meaning on a handshake. He doesn't have contracts with clients and operates on trust. So far, this has worked for him, but he's left himself wide open for risk. It would only take one incident to topple the business he's worked so hard to build. Many trainers are in this same position and don't even realize it.

As a trainer, you likely don't have unlimited resources to spend on legal fees for lawsuits. But sometimes, you'll find that you're dealing with a wealthy client who has significantly more resources than you do and may choose to use litigation against you, knowing you can't defend yourself the same way they can. If these clients wanted to, they could litigate you into financial ruin.

If you're in business long enough in any industry, you will encounter someone who (whether for a legitimate reason or not) has a disagreement with you. When it comes to legal disputes, it's not if; it's when.

You can't control how other people act and react, but you can take proactive measures to get where you want to go.

To protect yourself from liability, you need the three-legged stool of protection:

1. Insurance
2. Contracts
3. Incorporation

If you remove one leg from a three-legged stool, the stool will fall over. Likewise, you won't be fully protected if you're missing just one of these three elements.

The majority of trainers I meet are often inadequately insured. They typically hold a liability coverage of one million dollars, which may not be sufficient for comprehensive protection. The amount of insurance necessary varies based on their specific circumstances, so it is advisable to consult both an equine law attorney and an insurance representative to determine the most suitable insurance coverage.

Many trainers I speak with are unaware that California has no equine activity liability law. California-based trainers who travel to other states for competitions may see signs or waivers regarding the Equine Activity Liability Act and assume it applies to them. However, this is not the case if you operate from California. Consequently, it becomes even more crucial for California-based trainers to meticulously draft contracts to protect their business interests.

We have seen many trainers resort to using Liability Release Waivers found online or "borrowed" from friends. However, these contracts often do not align with California law. The issue with such agreements is that they are not tailored to the specific needs of the trainer since they were initially drafted for someone else, potentially resulting in a lack of complete protection.

On numerous occasions, we've received calls from trainers about Liability Release Waivers they've been utilizing for years. However, upon reviewing these documents, we often find that they were originally drafted to conform to the laws of a different state. Many contracts have been passed around and modified so many times that they end up as cobbled-together "Frankenstein" contracts that make little sense legally.

Bridging Expectations: The Art of Crafting Training Agreements with Clients

A significant number of trainers lack formal training agreements with their clients. From the trainer's perspective, the absence of a contract can pose a greater risk to them than it might to their clients.

A training contract is an agreement between trainers and clients, defining duties and expectations for both sides. In the absence of such contracts, trainers may encounter several issues, one notable problem being billing—how do you proceed with collecting payment from a client when there is no written understanding regarding the payment procedure?

A Note on Billing

It is good business practice to make sure your clients are billed every month. You should break down the bill, so your client understands exactly what they are paying for–transparency is key. We have worked on multiple cases of billing disputes that could have been avoided with a proper invoice.

Emmett was a passionate horse trainer who had been teaching children to ride for many years. He was beloved in the community for his devotion to his craft and the exemplary training he provided to both horses and their owners. He had one significant rule for conducting business - he never insisted on any formal contracts with his clients. He believed in trust, respect, and good faith.

Mr. Huntington approached Emmett to train his prized jumper for an upcoming horse show. Thrilled at the opportunity, Emmett put all his energy into the horse's training to prepare for the upcoming show.

A week before the show, Mr. Huntington abruptly canceled his horse's participation in the show, as it turned out he had a work conflict and would not be able to be there to watch. Emmett was surprised and reminded him of the expenses he had already incurred in anticipation of the event - transportation fees, hotel bookings, and payments made in advance to grooms and braiders. However, Mr. Huntington shrugged it off, believing that he owed Emmett nothing since they were no longer attending.

Emmett was stuck. With no contract in place, he was unable to demand reimbursement. The financial loss was significant and took a toll on his small business. It was a hard lesson learned for Emmett, one that he would remember for the rest of his training career.

This unfortunate event led Emmett to change his old approach. He sought professional help from an equine attorney and created a comprehensive training contract for his services. The contract outlined all responsibilities and expectations, including specific provisions about horse show attendance. It stated that clients were liable for horse show costs unless they canceled before the close of the show entries.

From that day forward, Emmett's business ran smoother than ever. The unfortunate incident with Mr. Huntington served as a wake-up call. The clarity provided by the contract saved him from future misunderstandings and possible financial losses.

A poorly drafted contract is no better than a handshake.

I always recommend that trainers have contracts with alternative dispute resolution language so they can hopefully settle disputes more cost-effectively than going to court. Mediation levels the playing field with your very wealthy clients. It's no longer about who can outspend the other party in litigation.

Also, it's important to note that even if you have a good chance of winning your court case, you may not win enough money to cover your attorney fees, so you'd have a net loss. You can include attorney fee provisions in your contract, but it's up to the discretion of the judge to award them. If there's a mediation provision in your trainer contract, it's required that both parties go to mediation before filing a lawsuit. At our firm, we have a very high success rate of settlement at mediation–as a result, we are often able to save our clients a significant amount of money.

Choosing the right mediator...

The effectiveness of mediators can vary widely. Certain mediators offer mediation as only one facet of their practice, and as they are not exclusively mediators, their proficiency might not be as high. In contrast, some mediators are extremely competent because their professional focus is mediation. Our experience suggests that many mediators claiming to understand the horse industry often lack comprehensive knowledge in this area. It would be more advantageous to select a mediator who, while possibly lacking specific knowledge of the horse industry, has a strong track record in resolving cases. This way, your equine attorney can provide the necessary insight into the nuances of the horse industry, facilitating an informed mediation process.

A good trainer's contract will include...

A well-crafted contract between a horse trainer and their customer should cover all essential aspects of their relationship and be clear on both parties' expectations, responsibilities, and liabilities. Here are some components that should be included:

Services to be Provided: The contract should clearly outline the trainer's services. This could include details of the training plan, the type of training, the number of lessons per week, and number of training rides included per week.

Fees and Payment Terms: The contract should clearly define the cost of services, payment schedule, method of payment, what happens if a payment is late or missed, and whether or how often the trainer will be sending invoices.

Horse Show Attendance: If applicable, details about horse show participation, including who pays for related costs (transportation, accommodation, grooming, etc.), and the consequences of last-minute cancellations, should be included.

Emergency Veterinary Care: The contract should detail the protocol for emergency veterinary care, including who is authorized to make decisions when the client cannot be reached and who is responsible for associated costs.

An Exit Plan/Termination Clause: The contract should include detailed conditions under which the agreement can be terminated by either party and how much notice needs to be given.

Equipment/Tack Left After Termination: How long does a trainer have to store someone's saddle or other equipment after the client has terminated the contract?

Dispute Resolution: The contract should outline the process for resolving any disagreements that may arise, such as mediation or arbitration.

Miscellaneous Provisions: These might include the trainer's right to use photographs of a horse or rider in advertising, whether the client can take lessons with other trainers, and if the horse can be ridden by other students when the client is out of town for a prolonged period of time.

The above list is not exhaustive, and the specifics may vary depending on the circumstances. It's always best to consult with an attorney or legal expert when drafting any legal contract you will use to protect yourself.

Checklist for Removing a Client (for Trainers or Stable Managers)

☑ Review your contract. Hopefully, you have a training or boarding contract with your client that specifies how much notice you have to give to ask someone to leave. If you don't, you need to get one of those drafted post haste.

☑ Invoices and Payments. Review if the client you are asking to leave owes you any money. If they do, ask for it to be paid BEFORE you ask them to leave. In my experience, the chances of getting paid as a stable or trainer once you have asked someone to leave are very low.

What to Do When a Boarder Won't Leave

If you board horses, you may find that it is time to ask a boarder to leave your facility, yet they resist. Their reasons could range from difficulty finding another suitable boarding location to simply being unwilling to move.

To protect yourself and minimize any conflict, your boarding or training agreement should include an exit protocol.

Worker Misclassification

Employment law could be a book all on its own. Below, we will briefly discuss a few employment law scenarios that trainers should be looking for, but if you think you might have an employment law issue, we highly recommend you contact an attorney immediately.

Trainers often misclassify workers by calling them independent contractors when they're really employees. This misclassification isn't intentional—most trainers simply haven't been educated on the legal difference between employees and independent contractors. They may have read online or been told that having an independent contractor agreement makes someone an independent contractor, but that is often false. If someone comes to work for you at a scheduled time and is treated like an employee, there is a very high chance that the State of California will consider them an employee even if they have an independent contractor agreement. **This means you may unknowingly violate employment laws because you believe you only have independent contractors.**

In California, worker's compensation insurance for horse-related activities is expensive, and you're required to have it if you have employees. Some trainers may be unable to afford payroll and worker's compensation, and they've been told that classifying employees as independent contractors is an easy way to save money. However, these trainers haven't been warned that misclassifying workers has civil and criminal penalties. Not only can you be sued, but you could go to jail.

Thomas had a robust horse training business with a dedicated team of grooms who were employed as his employees and for whom he had dutifully paid worker's compensation insurance.

One summer, Thomas and his team attended a horse show. A long-standing practice in the industry was that grooms from different stables occasionally help each other during the show. Abiding by this common practice, Thomas's grooms hired a few extra hands from another stable for half a day to assist with unloading horses from Thomas's horse trailer.

Thomas knew of this practice at horse shows, but he failed to consider the potential legal risks tied to these friendships. Like many trainers, the prevalence of this practice had desensitized him to its potential hazards.

Nearly a year after the horse show, an unexpected claim shook Thomas's world. One of the temporary grooms, who had assisted his team that day, claimed to have injured his shoulder while unloading Thomas's horses. The man claimed his shoulder injury was so severe that he could no longer work.

Thomas had no recollection of any accidents that day, nor had there been any immediate reports of injuries. However, the lack of a formal contract with the temporary groom left him vulnerable to the claim. The man's claim was against Thomas's worker's compensation insurance, and the lack of formal

EMPOWERING TRAINERS - STRATEGIES FOR PROTECTING YOURSELF AND YOUR CLIENTS | 125

paperwork meant he had little legal ground to refute it. Thomas ended up being dragged into a year-long lawsuit.

If you can't afford to classify your workers properly and have the proper worker's compensation insurance, you likely shouldn't be in business because the potential risks are significant.

Mitigating Risks with Attorney-Drafted Sales & Lease Contracts And What You As A Trainer Need To Know

Leasing a horse isn't like leasing a car. If you're leasing a car and it breaks, you can take it to a mechanic and get it fixed. If you're leasing a horse and it has an injury that can never be fixed, what happens? Who's responsible? Can the person leasing the horse return it early if it gets hurt? These are just a few of the questions that are often not thought through when an owner considers leasing out their horse. What happens if the horse gets injured in month one, and someone is now responsible for eleven months of rehabbing the horse? If a lessee is new to the industry, they likely won't even understand what is involved with rehabbing an injured horse. But if they have worked with an equine attorney ahead of time, who has explained this to them, and then drafted a lease agreement that is clear and unambiguous, they are more likely to understand the risks and obligations.

In 2010, Business and Professions Code §19525 was passed in California, which requires the written disclosure of trainer's or agent's commissions for any commission over $500. It also requires the written disclosure of dual agencies (i.e. when a trainer is acting on behalf of both the buyer and the seller). As a trainer, if a horse is being sold from one client to the other in your barn, it has to be disclosed in the sales contract that you were acting as a dual agent. Violating this statute comes with the penalty of treble damages, which is three times the amount of damages. If you're selling a $200,000 horse, you could potentially be looking at significant damages if you violate the commission disclosure law. This disclosure needs to be written in every bill of sale.

The code uses the language "sale or transfer of a horse," so there can be a gray area on whether or not a lease is considered a transfer, though one could argue that a lease is a transfer. The purpose of the law is to provide transparency, so I recommend that my clients include this disclosure on leases as well.

Many times, trainers believe they can draft sales or lease contracts on their own, unaware of the potential risks they are exposing themselves and their clients to. I often encounter DIY lease and sales contracts with significant gaps. DIY contracts often comprise a patchwork of legal phrases that ultimately don't work well together. The drafter, lacking legal expertise, usually doesn't fully understand the implications of these terms. The document might appear convincing to an untrained observer, yet it would likely not withstand legal scrutiny in court.

The risks are high when legal documents are drafted without professional legal guidance. The perceived savings in avoiding lawyer fees could easily be overshadowed by the costs of a legal dispute down the line. It's better to get it right from the start with the help of a qualified equine attorney.

The Advantages of Working With a Lawyer

There are many advantages to working with a lawyer when drafting legal contracts. The advantages differ depending upon the type of contract.

In California, ambiguous terms in a contract are often construed against the drafter. This can present significant challenges for a trainer who has drafted a sales or lease contract on behalf of a client without legal assistance. Misinterpretations or ambiguities in the contract could unintentionally disadvantage the trainer or their client.

In the context of trainers' contracts, one substantial benefit of working with a lawyer is their ability to foresee potential issues that you might not have encountered or even considered. Many clauses incorporated in our trainer contracts stem from real-world scenarios where trainers faced difficulties or financial losses. Our objective has always been to identify preventive measures against such future complications. With over 16 years of experience, we've compiled a comprehensive list of potential problems to mitigate.

The benefit of working with an experienced equine attorney is that, though you may be experiencing a problem for the first time, we've seen trainers encounter the same problem dozens of times before and know how to prevent it. Rather than learning the "hard way" from your own mistakes, you can learn from the mistakes of others that your attorney has worked with and prevent problems before they even occur.

Well-drafted contracts will also benefit your clients by providing transparency and clear expectations. Contracts can protect everyone involved if drafted properly, so it's a win-win situation for both parties. With well-written contracts, clients will be more likely to work with you and refer you because they know what the terms of your relationship will be and can trust you.

Preventing loss is much less expensive than dealing with a problem after it has occurred. And many problems can be easily avoided by having a contract in place. A recent case illustrates that situation:

Emma was a devoted horse trainer known in her community for her compassion and commitment towards her equine companions. One day, she was faced with a situation that left her emotionally shattered and financially strained. Magic, a horse under her care, fell gravely ill. Emma's instincts told her something was wrong, and she wanted to call a veterinarian immediately. However, the owner, Sara, was out of town, and Emma had to speak to her on the phone. Sara, since she was not there, preferred a more cautious approach, deciding to wait and monitor the horse's condition.

Emma did not have a training or boarding agreement with Sara that authorized her to call the veterinarian in emergency situations, as their arrangement had been established on good faith and handshakes. Thus, despite her concerns, Emma was forced to respect Sara's decision.

Tragically, Magic's condition deteriorated rapidly, and he passed away within 24 hours. Emma found herself in an untenable situation, held accountable for a substantial sum, as she was the one who had Magic under her care when he died. Sara blamed Emma for not explaining how sick the horse was.

In hindsight, if a contract had been in place that authorized Emma to summon a veterinarian on Sara's behalf, the outcome might have been different. Magic could have received timely veterinary attention, potentially saving his life, and Emma wouldn't have been left dealing with such a substantial liability.

Having an attorney draft a contract does take a financial investment, but it has immense value. If you can communicate this value to your horse owner clients, they'll never want to hire a trainer without a contract again.

When you begin a relationship with an equine attorney, they can ensure that you reach out to clients every few years and adjust the contract slightly to reflect updates over time. You won't have to worry about remembering to do this because your attorney will keep track of changes in the law or your situation that would necessitate updating contracts, provided you are on a subscription plan with the attorney.

And if you have a continued relationship with an attorney, then when something goes wrong, you already have a trusted advisor who knows your business and can support you.

An attorney may know the law and be a great lawyer, but if they don't understand the horse industry, there will be a huge gap in their experience, leaving you at a disadvantage. To be successful, you need an attorney with the intersection of legal expertise and industry knowledge.

A Note About Co-Ownership With Your Clients

Having a client who wants to bolster your career by purchasing a horse for you might initially seem like a wonderful opportunity. However, without a written agreement, this seemingly kind gesture can lead to complications down the road. Such arrangements can work smoothly, provided there's a well-articulated contract that sets clear expectations and establishes a comprehensive exit plan.

By detailing the exit plan, you pave the way for a less stressful and drama-free experience that won't negatively impact your business or potentially land you in court if the relationship ends. Even in situations where litigation hasn't occurred, I've encountered numerous cases where trainers have lost valuable clients due to poorly executed co-ownership agreements.

These types of scenarios arise when both parties hold different expectations about the arrangement. To prevent such misalignments, a well-crafted contract is essential. It not only safeguards your professional relationships but also ensures the longevity and success of your business.

The Top 10 Tips for Trainers

1. Insurance (Have the right type…and enough of it)

2. Have Written Sales and Lease Agreements

3. Comply with Disclosure of Commissions

4. Have a well-drafted Release of Liability/Assumption of Risk Waiver

5. Have a written Trainer Contract

6. Have a written Tack & Equipment Policy

7. Don't enter into co-ownership agreements with clients unless you are well protected contractually

8. Classify employees correctly

9. Know USEF, FEI, and Safe Sport rules

10. Take rider safety precautions to ensure everyone has a safe and fun time.

CHAPTER 11

Family Offices

Family offices are private wealth management advisory firms that serve high-net-worth families and investors. They often manage the family's wealth, legacy, investments, and day-to-day administrative tasks. When a family office ends up involved in the horse industry, it is generally because the family has a personal interest or passion for this niche industry.

The horse industry encompasses a wide range of activities, such as racing, breeding, equestrian sports, and recreational riding. It requires substantial knowledge and experience to successfully navigate due to its complex nature and the significant capital investment often required. When the personal and professional spheres of the family collide, as in the story of Rachel below, it can result in unique challenges and considerations.

Rachel runs a family office for a high-net-worth family, the Johnsons, who have recently acquired horses and built a stable on their multimillion-dollar property. Mrs. Johnson hosts a fundraising gala at the home and takes a few guests into the stable to show them her horses. One of the horses gets scared and bites a guest, who files a lawsuit.

Rachel is frustrated–she thought the family owning horses would be simple, and she didn't foresee an incident like this. Now, the family is facing a lawsuit that could threaten their assets and provide negative publicity. Rachel is sure she could have taken action to prevent this situation, but because she comes from the world of finance and knows next to nothing about horses, she wasn't aware that this could even be a situation she would need to take preventative measures against. If Rachel had consulted an equine attorney when the family bought their first horse, she and the family may have avoided this lawsuit.

Risk Management

Risk management is one of the top priorities of a family office when they call our office. Much like Lisa and John from Chapter One, the family office managers we work with are often new to the industry and have no horse knowledge. So, they face the same risks as Lisa and John but on a much larger scale.

From a financial perspective, the biggest risk anyone in the horse industry faces, including the family office, is the risk that a horse they own will injure or kill a person, and they will become involved in a public, messy, and expensive lawsuit. Family offices are often seen as a target for lawsuits because they have deep pockets. Consequently, there might be individuals seeking to bring a lawsuit against them or intentionally exploit the family office client with the aim of securing monetary gains. As the family office manager, it's essential to do everything in your power to minimize the family's risk and protect them upfront from this type of behavior.

Unknown liability exposure for the family can arise in many different ways, especially if the family owns a horse property. An equine attorney can educate the family office manager on the risks and minimize them as situations arise.

For example, if the family wants to have a young daughter's friends over to ride horses, what liability exposure could arise? What steps can they take ahead of time to ensure this can be done safely and responsibly?

Imagine the family is hosting a large crowd over for a birthday party—how will they ensure no one interacts with the horses? Maybe the family wants their guests to be able to interact with the horses. What policies can they put in place to ensure their employees can help non-riders behave safely around the horses?

We had one client who wanted to throw a large black-tie event in a barn. The guests weren't interacting with horses, so we didn't need them to sign the release of liability, but we ensured that employees guided guests to the right areas in the barn so they were kept safely away from the horses.

Another way family offices may unknowingly be exposed to risk is in employment. If the family has its own private trainer or grooms, it often needs to ensure that they have adequate worker's compensation insurance and proper employee protocols in place.

To mitigate potential liability exposure and threats arising from employees, it's crucial for a family office to deploy insurance and legal contracts meticulously drafted by an attorney. While a trainer might require liability insurance coverage of three to five million dollars, the assets owned by a family office significantly exceed this, necessitating a comprehensive review by your legal and insurance advisors to determine the right insurance coverage for optimum protection. To safeguard against employment-related liabilities, it's essential to correctly classify all employees and strictly adhere to all workers' compensation regulations.

Expertise Management and Exit Plans

Navigating the horse industry requires an understanding of numerous factors, including horse care, breeding, training, and competition rules to name a few. This requires a significant time investment and often necessitates building relationships with industry experts. Family offices often have private agreements with trainers or other vendors, which means they need a good strategy to manage these relationships and a solid exit plan.

If a family has 5-10 horses with the same trainer, they are a huge source of income for that trainer. This puts a lot of pressure on the relationship with the trainer. If they end the working relationship, this trainer's business will be at risk, which can be highly emotional for the trainer. And when people get emotional, that's often when legal trouble can occur...

Because of this, all family office managers (and even those with only one horse) need to have a clear exit plan spelled out in a contract that both parties agree to before beginning the relationship. Sometimes, relationships with trainers end on good terms, and sometimes, they do not. The family might understand that moving to a new trainer would deal a large financial blow to their current trainer, but they still need to be able to move on. With a well-drafted written agreement, the family can ensure this transition occurs gracefully. The trainer may still have strong emotions about the family leaving, but with expectations set up front, they'll know the terms of the relationship and won't take out their frustrations via a lawsuit.

But when you don't set expectations up front, you leave room for people to set unrealistic expectations. A trainer may build their livelihood around your family, assuming that you'll be a client for a long time and come to depend on your horses as the sole source of their income. Imagine how you'd react if someone was threatening 10% of your income. Now, imagine how you'd react if someone was threatening 80%-90% of your income. It's natural for a trainer to be upset and want to sue in this situation, but this is a mess that can be avoided by setting expectations before beginning the relationship.

Working with an equine attorney who is well-versed in both the legal dimensions as well as the interpersonal dynamics between the trainer and the family can be beneficial, allowing the attorney to advise the family office and help draft a contract that prevents problems ahead of time by making sure everyone is on the same page.

Privacy

Maintaining the privacy of family matters is often a top priority for the family office manager. Including confidentiality clauses in sales and lease agreements and agreements with trainers and other vendors is critical to ensure a family's private affairs are not aired ringside at a horse show.

Earlier in the book, we discussed the value of mediation for every contract. The same ideas hold true for the family office. However, it is critical that the contract specifies that the mediation be confidential. If mediation fails, most family offices would be best suited by having mandatory arbitration as opposed to a lawsuit in Superior Court. All lawsuits brought in Superior Court are public record; bringing a matter before an arbitrator is not public and thus is a way to ensure privacy for the family.

Protecting Your Client from Being a Target

Sometimes, those in the equine industry who interact with family offices view them as a source of abundant wealth that could be exploited. The changes to Business and Professions Code §19525 came about because a wealthy businessman involved in the horse industry was seen as a target, and his trainers charged double and even triple commissions on his purchases of racehorses, and the trainers thought they could get away with it because he had deep pockets.

Your family office may be pressured into buying horses, which could lead to buying an inappropriate or injured horse due to being rushed through the purchasing process. For a family office, sales and leases are often more complex and carry larger risks because the family may be buying more horses or more expensive horses than the average consumer.

Transparency is a crucial defense in safeguarding family office clients from becoming targets. This transparency can be achieved through carefully drafted contracts that leave no room for misconceptions or manipulations. This can instill a sense of trust and clarity between all parties involved, fostering healthier business relationships, and these contracts act as legal barriers, deterring potential exploitation by outlining the consequences of violations. With meticulous planning and legal guidance, a well-drafted contract promotes transparency, mitigates risks, and ultimately protects the family office client from falling prey to ill-intentioned schemes.

Emotional Involvement and the Balance of Interests

Unlike typical investments, investing in the horse industry often carries a higher degree of emotional involvement. This is especially true if family members are personally involved in equestrian activities or are passionate about horses. Emotions can sometimes cloud objective decision-making, leading to unwise financial decisions. We often counsel clients to take a step back from the transaction and to examine it from a business perspective. It is all too easy to get wrapped up in the moment and consider an overpriced horse purchase for your child due to its immediate gratification and temporary problem-solving nature. However, letting emotions drive these decisions can bring about greater complications in the future. By working with an equine attorney, our family office clients often learn to pause, and we can help them to step back and look at the transaction objectively and then make a decision. The decision may still be the same, but if the client has had an opportunity to pause, they know the risks when making the decision.

Final Considerations

When a family office becomes involved in the horse industry, it's a significant step that involves a myriad of challenges and considerations that they likely have not faced before. The venture can be fulfilling and rewarding but also poses unique risks and complexities that the family office must be equipped to handle. Often, the family office is made up of a team of people with no horse background to support the family. They may have fantastic lawyers, but if they aren't familiar with the horse industry, there is certain information they will not know. Having an equine lawyer to advise them will allow them to help the family make informed decisions.

Often, people think the more money they spend in the industry, the better results they'll get. But more money won't get better results if you're putting it into the wrong trainer, the wrong horses, or doing it without a strategic plan and a team that understands the horse industry and related laws. It doesn't matter how much money you have if you start off in the wrong direction, so it's best to work with a trusted advisor who can set you on the right path from the beginning rather than try to fix problems when they come up.

CHAPTER 12

Horse Associations & Governing Bodies

Attorneys play a vital role in assisting horse associations or the governing bodies of equestrian sports in various ways. Our office works closely with several different horse associations helping them to protect the organization as a whole and their members to make sure they have longevity within the horse industry.

Governance and Ethics

An attorney can provide guidance on governance issues, such as developing bylaws, resolving board disputes, ensuring regulatory compliance, and navigating the nuances of nonprofit law if the association is a nonprofit entity. Attorneys can help to establish codes of conduct and enforce ethical guidelines. They can also counsel on the structure and responsibilities of the board of directors and conflicts of interest.

Many horse associations were created years ago, and in many cases, their bylaws, articles of organization, and rules have not undergone updates or revisions in recent years. These documents govern the operation of the associations and serve

142 | BLUE RIBBON LAW

as a foundation for their structure and procedures. Changes in society, technology, and the equestrian industry itself may necessitate modifications in these foundational texts. The bylaws and rules might not reflect current best practices or the modern realities of the horse world, thus potentially hindering the association's adaptability to the current context.

When there's a dispute within a horse association, the first step is to look at the bylaws, which often the board members find outdated. We've had situations where associations could not locate the original bylaws because the organization was created four decades ago before computers existed... Most organizations tend to keep rules up to date but don't change bylaws to reflect the rules. We have found that attorneys without knowledge of the horse industry often drafted the bylaws. The members of the organization's executive offices rarely look at the bylaws until there is an issue that the bylaws need to resolve.

In one case, two organizations merged and simply stapled their two sets of bylaws together, which were over a decade old. This merged organization did not update these makeshift bylaws until there was a major dispute confronting the organization. When the organization looked at the stapled-together bylaws, they discovered that the original, separate organizations had some bylaws that contradicted each other. The members of the organization argued over which set of bylaws should be honored in the dispute. Yet this confusion and chaos could have been easily prevented when the organizations merged.

Dispute Resolution

Conflicts can arise in any organization, ranging from contract disputes between the association and its members to disputes with sponsors and employee issues. An equine attorney can assist in resolving these disputes through negotiation, mediation, or court proceedings if necessary.

When an issue arises, an attorney will look at what remedies are possible and help the association decide the best course of action. When there are disputes between members of an organization, if the bylaws are well drafted, there are often ways compliant with the bylaws for the issue to be adjudicated with a hearing by the organization. This hearing procedure is loosely governed by California law. Generally, at the hearing, an attorney can represent the organization and protect the organization from legal challenges after the hearing. In some cases, if an association violates a rule, the incident may be taken to state court.

Disputes between members over matters such as conduct at a horse show can be filled with emotion… If these conflicts go far enough, they can be destructive to the horse association. Horse associations are often underfunded, and one lawsuit that gets out of hand could bankrupt the organization.

Individual members within a horse association are often wealthy and can afford expensive legal fees, whereas the horse association itself may not have the funds for a lawsuit. Even if the organization could win the lawsuit, it may have a net loss in legal fees. We've seen organizations almost destroyed over conflicts between members. When these conflicts arise, organizations that have bylaws preventing a lawsuit are more likely to survive.

Pegasus Horse Association was an organization founded many years ago. It was the governing body that regulated all matters related to horse breeding, competition, and registration, and it became embroiled in a lengthy debate between its members Sam and Maria.

Glorious Freedom was a stunning bay stallion, hailing from a long line of celebrated champions. At the heart of the controversy was a lingering question, "Did Glorious Freedom have a rare genetic condition that would impact not only his competitive performance but also his ability to pass on his traits to future generations?"

On one side of the debate was Maria, the owner of Glorious Freedom, and on the other side was Sam, whose family was deeply rooted in the equestrian world. Maria argued that Glorious Freedom was in perfect health. She pointed to his numerous competition wins, robust health, and glowing veterinarian recommendations as proof of her claim.

Sam, with the help of Dr. Sylvia Matthews, a leading equine geneticist, believed Glorious Freedom carried a rare genetic disorder. Although asymptomatic in the horse, this disorder was thought to produce debilitating effects in its offspring. The evidence, however, was circumstantial at best. Only a tiny percentage of Glorious Freedom's offspring exhibited symptoms, and no definitive genetic test existed yet to establish the link conclusively.

The debate raged on for months, both sides producing evidence and counter-evidence, expert witnesses, and testimony. Accusations and animosity festered, the environment becoming more hostile as the stakes rose and the risks of the dispute destroying the association grew. In the end, Pegasus Horse Association decided that the matter could only be resolved through a formal hearing.

A three-member panel was convened, composed of three board members who were experts in their own right – a seasoned horse breeder, a veterinary medical expert, and a genetic scientist. The case of Glorious Freedom was presented in all its complexity, the hearing taking several days to ensure all arguments and evidence were thoroughly examined.

The panel diligently dissected every claim, every piece of evidence, and every testimony. After days of deliberation, they finally arrived at a decision. As Dr. Matthews had claimed, Glorious Freedom was a carrier of the rare genetic condition. However, it was also established that the situation was less detrimental than previously assumed. It was a latent trait that would not necessarily manifest in all offspring, and its debilitating effects could be mitigated with early detection and proper care. Therefore, Glorious Freedom should be allowed to continue to stand as a Stallion with its permitted offspring to be registered with Pegasus Horse Association.

Because Pegasus Horse Association had well-drafted bylaws and rules and the counsel of an attorney throughout the whole saga, the association navigated the issue and devised a solution that avoided anyone having to file a lawsuit. Ensuring that an association's bylaws and rules include dispute resolution language can be critical for protecting both the association itself and the organization's leaders who are often volunteers.

Contractual Matters

Horse associations often enter into various contracts - with employees, vendors, event participants, sponsors, etc. An attorney can help draft, review, and negotiate these contracts to protect the association's interests. Throughout this book, we have discussed the importance of avoiding DIY contracts, and this principle holds for horse associations, too. However, the risks associated with errors in contract drafting are often amplified in such cases. For instance, a poorly drafted sponsorship agreement could impact not only the association itself but all the members as well.

Risk Management

Attorneys can assist a horse association in identifying and mitigating legal risks that could potentially harm the association. This involves a comprehensive understanding of the specific legal landscape, current laws, and the horse industry itself. The attorney can review the association's current operations, identifying areas of potential risk. Once these areas are identified, the attorney can recommend strategies to mitigate those risks, ensuring the association operates within legal bounds.

Insurance coverage is another important aspect where attorneys can provide valuable advice to a horse association. Many types of insurance coverage might be relevant to a horse association, such as liability insurance, board of directors insurance, property insurance, and accident insurance for participants, to name a few. An attorney can help an association understand what types of coverage are needed based on the nature of its activities. Moreover, they can assist in negotiating the terms of the insurance contracts, ensuring the association gets the most comprehensive coverage at the most reasonable price.

Implementing safety procedures is another critical area where legal advice is essential to aid the association in risk management. These procedures help ensure the well-being of all involved parties, from participants to staff and horses. Attorneys can advise on best practices for safety, help design protocols and procedures, and provide training to staff on how to adhere to these standards. Legal guidance can ensure these safety measures are effective and comply with all relevant regulations.

Another area where an attorney's expertise can also significantly protect a horse association is by drafting waivers and release forms. These documents are legal contracts that can limit the association's liability in the event of an accident or injury.

Education

Often, the board members of a horse association are people in the community who believe in the association and want to see it thrive. Many times, they have not been on other boards and do not have a legal background. When an association works with an equine attorney, that attorney can educate the board members on all of the various legal requirements of being on a board, including their legal rights and responsibilities, and provide updates on changes in relevant laws. If a dispute arises, the board members already know they have someone to turn to who is looking out for the best interest of the horse association.

Final Thoughts

Equine attorneys play a crucial role in horse associations' operational success and legal compliance. With their legal expertise, they can provide guidance on matters related to governance and ethics, dispute resolution, contracts, and risk management, ensuring that these organizations operate within the legal frameworks. They can assist in understanding and interpreting complex legal regulations that often intertwine with the activities of horse associations, ensuring compliance and avoiding costly legal issues. By foreseeing and mitigating legal risks, they protect the horse associations from potential lawsuits and contribute to a stable and safer environment for the members and the association itself.

CONCLUSION

Now that you've read this book, my hope is that you're aware that you are exposed to liability. By simply doing things "the way it's always been done" in the equestrian industry, you have unknowingly left yourself open to the risk of a lawsuit, a financial loss, or a stressful conflict with another party.

You now have clarity about the risks you face and the steps you can take to protect yourself before any incident occurs. And if an incident does occur, you understand the importance of seeking legal guidance rather than trying to work it out with a "handshake" or "doing things the way they've always been done." If you do begin a relationship with an attorney, you know the right questions to ask so you can make informed choices and avoid common pitfalls.

Armed with your new knowledge, there is no better time than today to take action to protect yourself before an incident occurs.

With a very small investment of time, energy, and money, you can protect yourself by seeking advice from an equine attorney. Once you do this and implement protective measures, you'll no longer feel a threat hanging over your head or hiding around a corner.

You can continue your involvement in the industry with peace of mind, knowing that you've done everything in your power to prevent catastrophe. Without fear, stress, and uncertainty, you can focus on growing your business, becoming a better rider, or enjoying life on the horse property of your dreams. This industry has the power to bring great joy to your life when you can participate in it without apprehension.

But anyone who fails to take action will continue to be exposed to significant risk…and there is no way of knowing the scale of that risk. It could be tremendous or minor—and it's difficult to know for sure until it's too late. When people leave risk hanging over them, unguarded, there will always be fear in the back of their minds: "What if this transaction doesn't go according to plan? What if my horse causes an accident? What will happen to my business if I'm sued?" I don't want you to regret the simple actions you could have taken to avoid disaster.

As you discovered in this book, there are countless stories of misfortune and tragedy that arose from a lack of legal protections. Most of these stories did not have to end the way they did. It's my mission to encourage everyone involved in the horse industry to assess their risks and implement protections so they are as protected as they can be and can instead experience the many benefits of being involved in the equestrian community.

If you are ready to shield yourself from risk, or just have questions and would like to speak to an attorney about the risks you face we are happy to help. Scan the QR code on the next page and book a call with our team today.

https://www.blueribbonlaw.com/

Bonus Gift

As our gift to you, we've created 5 checklists that you can download and take with you as you head back out to the barn. Scan the QR code that applies to your situation, or scan them all and get all five lists!

For Horse Owners https://BlueRibbonLaw.com/horseowner-checklist	
For Horse Property Owners https://BlueRibbonLaw.com/horseproperty-checklist	
For Trainers https://BlueRibbonLaw.com/trainer-checklist	

For Family Offices https://BlueRibbonLaw.com/familyoffice-checklist	
For Horse Association https://BlueRibbonLaw.com/association-checklist	

Additional Resources

#1. YouTube - I post informative videos on key legal issues facing people in the horse industry on my YouTube Channel. Tune in at https://BlueRibbonLaw.com/YouTube

#2. Monthly Email Insights - I share the latest legal insights and trends in the horse industry by email. Subscribe at https://BlueRibbonLaw.com/newsletter

ABOUT THE AUTHOR

Polly Hey, a distinguished equine attorney and lifelong equestrian, co-founded Hey & Hey in 2006, specializing exclusively in equine law. Licensed in California and Tennessee, she combines her legal expertise with a deep understanding of equine matters, offering unparalleled advice to her clients. Raised as a rider, Polly is a respected member of numerous equestrian associations, and she is dedicated to advancing equine education, often delivering lectures and providing resources to empower horse enthusiasts. Her relentless advocacy and integrity make her a trusted advisor in the equestrian community.

Made in the USA
Las Vegas, NV
19 November 2023

81196273R00085